D0811116

Afloat

Afloat

A Memoir

DANIE COUCHMAN

Illustrations by Eleanor Taylor

Hardie Grant

QUADRILLE

Publishing Director Sarah Lavelle
Commissioning Editor Susannah Otter
Copy Editor Sally Somers
Designer Gemma Hayden
Illustrator Eleanor Taylor
Production Director Vincent Smith
Production Controller Sinead Hering

Published in 2019 by Quadrille, an imprint of
Hardie Grant Publishing

Quadrille
52–54 Southwark Street
London SE1 1UN
quadrille.com

Cataloguing in Publication Data: a catalogue record for this
book is available from the British Library.

ISBN 978 1 78713 348 8

Printed in Spain

For the flotilla and my family, with lots of love

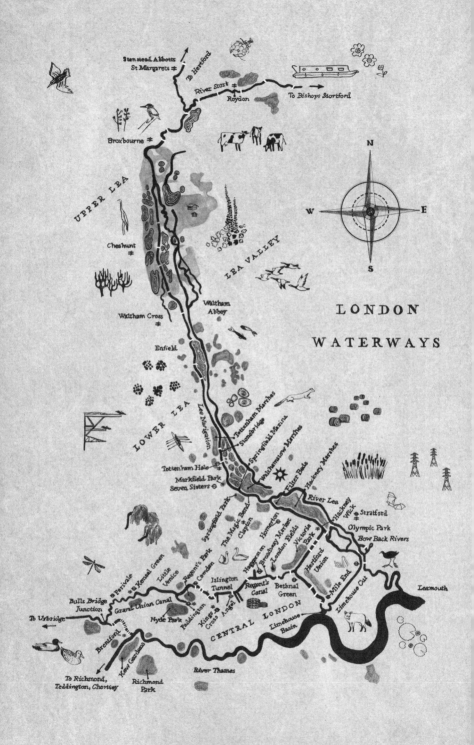

CONTENTS

PROLOGUE

When I was eleven, I stood at the top of the steep staircase with all the black and white photos Dad had taken of my younger brother Ben and me hanging along the walls. I was looking down at the front door, where Dad stood holding a brown leather suitcase, the type a kid being evacuated in the war might have had. He said goodbye. I knew, by the way he said it, what was happening, and through sobs begged him not to leave. But that was that. He was gone. Mum told me I found the number of the other woman and called her a bitch down the phone. I don't remember that bit.

Life had been good until that point. It had been nomadic, and we'd never stayed long enough in one place to be able to say that was where I was *from*, but I had loved the adventure. My mum told me that in the moments after I was born, my dad – young and lean – took me into his arms and showed me around the RAF hospital where I'd entered this world. Mum, twenty-five, small but strong, was left lying in the hospital bed exhausted and baby-less. I imagine her chocolate-brown permed hair looking wildly perfect, her cheeks beautifully blushed.

It was the summer of 1987, and we were in Germany where Dad had been posted with the British Army. We'd be there a short while before moving on again. We moved to two places in

England whilst Dad trained to become an Army photographer. Belgium would be next, where I'd rescue ducklings from the drain at the back of the garden, and the symbol above my coat peg at the local nursery where everyone spoke French was a smiling crescent moon. My little brother Ben was born. Three months later, Dad was posted to Belize in Central America for six months. He sent me drawings of jungles and sea creatures. Then, when I was five, on we went to Northern Ireland, to a town six miles west of the daily IRA bomb explosions, deadly gun battles and violence of a troubled Belfast. We lived on a street where the ends of rainbows landed, and I'd walk home from school with my friend Catherine and her older brothers, my voice quickly picking up their thick Northern Irish accents, with tiny pink seashells in my pocket that I'd stolen from a classroom. Standing on kitchen chairs so we could reach the gas hob, we'd heat up a tin of soup by ourselves for tea at their house.

Sometimes, men in camouflage with guns would run through our back garden where I'd secretly planted a magic bean. Mum would check under the car before driving and not stop at red lights, and Dad would not take the same route twice in a row. A piece of flint got stuck in my knee when I fell off my bike. I still have the scar. My classmates wrote me goodbye letters when we left for England, promising to always be my friends. The army kids in the British barracks that we moved to next tried to make me say my first swear words. They were different to the other children I'd met. Before, we'd always lived on civilian streets and had local friends. Here, all the kids knew each other, they moved together in one big unit, their mums were young, their dads all part of the same regiment. They were friendly, but more wild. One girl took my shoe and threw it in the bin. Another girl, who was younger than me and had a pet Staffordshire Bull Terrier that shadowed her wherever she went, went for a poo on the stairwell because she was locked out of home. My soft Irish voice stood out, and within a few days I was speaking with a harsh and exaggerated South London twang, dropping my Ts and Hs. Have became 'av, water became wa-er. I stole 20p pieces from the bits and bobs drawer to buy pick'n'mix for Ben and me from the corner shop where the school bus picked us up each morning, and my new best school friend, Pavan, lived above the post office.

Each time we moved, Dad went ahead, and Mum packed up the house, got us two little ones on a plane, and then into a new local school. By the time I was seven I'd lived in eight homes and four countries. We were itinerant, with never enough time to establish foundations. Like a hardy plant that can grow in the crevices of rocks, I grew up clinging on to whatever surface I could find. I learned to grab onto whatever solid ground there was, soaking up all the goodness that the new land had to offer before we moved on again. It made me adaptable. It was perhaps this life of transience and constant change that would later make me recklessly open to new experiences. Perhaps it was this life that led me to a watery world in search of adventure and belonging.

I

It was late May 2013 when I found the canal. I remember the air finally felt warm, and the trees lining London's streets had begun to blossom. I was twenty-five, and living in my seventeenth home: a house in Hackney that I shared with three men I didn't know, and a sofa-crasher. My room was small and came with a broken bed and an old used mattress which took up most of the space, and a small wardrobe. It was next to the shared bathroom and lounge, which had a big TV and fast Wifi. It was in a neighbourhood of cheap chicken shops, Afro hairdressers, late-night pubs and Victorian houses with multiple door numbers and bins out front. After bills, this home in East London cost me around £900 each month. I had lived in six homes in London in four years. When I first arrived in the city, not knowing anyone or anywhere, I lived in a house in Ealing with four women I hadn't met until the day I moved in. My tiny room overlooked railway tracks and a constant whizz of trains. The landlord wouldn't let me put up curtains or a shelf so I moved out quickly, into a two-bed flat in Shepherd's Bush, with a boyfriend ten years older than me who had a little girl who sometimes stayed with us. We shared the flat with a Spanish and a French girl about my age. The girls both worked nights in hotels so they cooked in the early hours of the morning, pans clattering. Live music and shouting from the bar below sounded up through the floorboards. I would step out onto a roof through the bedroom window and look out over the madness; screeching sirens and the constant rumbling drone of cars, street cleaners and rubbish trucks. Every night I slept with ear plugs in, every night my sleep was still disrupted. With no dining room or lounge, we ate breakfast and dinner in the bedroom. We moved out, and my boyfriend and I stretched our budget to live in a one-bed flat on a quieter street in Chiswick. After just a few months, the landlord decided to sell and told us we had to leave. We broke up. Then there was a flat with another girl I didn't know. At this one, the landlord would come by without warning to get things from his shed. Eventually I ended up in the house-share in Hackney. I felt an affinity for Hackney, far more than West London. My grandparents and great-grandparents had lived in East London, and something about the streets on this side of town made me feel more at home. They felt alive.

I, like more than half the people in the world, had found myself residing in a crowded city because of the work it offered. I worked as a voice-over artist. I would spend my days writing and recording TV continuity announcements for reality and entertainment channels, and voicing commercials for pop stars' new singles and albums, and promos for American kids' programmes. I was one of the busiest voice-over artists on my agent's books and, scared of losing out on any gigs, and not quite believing my luck, I said yes to everything. I barely took a break bar a couple of weeks' holiday a year. Hours were completely lost in the Tube, many metres beneath the city, as I journeyed to various recording studios all over London each day, crossing boroughs and different worlds. I felt the droplets of clamminess forming on my lower back as I was pushed deeper into the Tube carriage along with the influx of other passengers squeezing on.

I was just one of a mass of career-driven, transient city workers being swallowed up and submerged as another strong stream of bodies surged through fast-closing train doors. I'd slop amongst the tidal wave of urban humans, of all ages, cultures and wealth wedged in and engulfed in transit, standing silently amongst the noises of clattering carriages. Around five million passengers squashed up underground each day, standing as close to each other as lovers would, breathing in each others' hot caffeinated breath, being pushed and pulled around the city. Headphones blocking out the sound, phones screening out the world, electronics helping us to ignore the stranger's face inches from our own and to cope with the unnaturalness of a mass intrusion of personal space by such a density of people. Then, along with the cascade of humans, amounting to well over a billion passengers a year, I'd slosh out as fast as a kid from a water chute, rapidly taken through a collection of non-places and humanless ticket barriers, and pop up, blinking, mole-like for light and air on land, into the fast-flowing urban current. Sometimes, as I walked among the hordes of urbanites swarming the city and racing to work, becoming more angry and fierce, all just to pay for extortionate rent and holidays to escape, I'd think, *why are we all doing this?*

I often found the multitude of 24-7 options, endless entertainment, rapid pace and noise overwhelming and exhausting, but thrilling at the same time – always new, and full of promise. I hated it, I loved it. I was buzzing and yet unfulfilled. At night, I did everything London demands you do when you're in your early twenties and have not long arrived. I went to pubs, house parties, clubs, restaurants. I painted my nails, sporadically did yoga and dance classes, threw parties, fell for a succession of unsuitable men. I felt guilty or that I was missing out if I ever chose to have a night in, because everyone else was always doing something.

Amongst all the people and noise, I barely noticed the quiet discontentment crawling beneath my skin. It was only when I went to bed that I could hear it. The ache of dissatisfaction and the itch for change would feel more present. I needed to do something. I just didn't know what.

Spring's warmth hit me as I left the air-conditioned recording studio in Angel, the way the heat of a new country does when you step off a plane. I stopped and closed my eyes to feel it. *I'll walk home today*, I decided, and found myself veering off the bustling streets towards the Regent's Canal. I had discovered that going towards water in London could be a way to escape. The Thames path from Hammersmith to Richmond was one of my favourite places. I liked walking past its eighteenth-century riverside pubs with names like The Blue Anchor and The Old Ship. I would look at the tall red brick houses with window frames painted bright white and front gardens hidden behind hedges that overlooked the river, deciding which one I'd like to live in one day. I had found myself being drawn to London's waterways but I had never discovered this stretch of the Regent's Canal before. At Angel the slope down to the canal was so steep I had to walk slowly not to slip. When I arrived at the bottom I felt like I'd stepped into a different, timeless world. In front of me was a straight canal leading to a curved low bridge. Within the water, a mirrored sky and colourful, slim steel boats. On either side, framing the scene, weeping willows, tall trees and dark ivy. The trees felt greener than they should be, as if someone had turned up the colour saturation. I felt an unfamiliar sense of peace and calm. After five years of London-living my senses had become accustomed to buildings, roads, crowds, cars. In a single moment everything had changed. This world I had stumbled upon was of different proportions, on a different colour spectrum. I was suddenly reminded that nature existed, that I liked and missed it, that I once spent most of my days running around in it.

I followed the boats. They lined the canal in every shape and size; professionally painted and obviously DIY'd; beautified and battle wounded; waxed and never been washed. There were slim six-foot-wide narrowboats and boats twice the width; single moored and two abreast; roofs adorned with plant pots of well-fed flowers and never-watered dried blooms; smart folding bikes and rust buckets on wheels. I ducked beneath the bridge. Green algae scraps peeled off the slimy walls of a lock eight feet deep called City Road Lock, wet velvet ripping like an old felty stage curtain. *Ding ding ding.* A squad of lycra-clad speed-lovers on light road bikes flew past on the thin towpath, forcing me and the other walkers, pram pushers and dogs to dodge their wheels and hug the wall to avoid being hit. Grunting joggers dressed in body-hugging active wear, perfect ponytails swishing, came at me from the other direction. I matched the slower pace of the red-nosed and much smilier stout-looking man plodding in front of me, tin of beer in hand, following his casual footsteps on my way from Angel to Mare Street in Hackney. On my left were tower blocks and tired playgrounds, and sleeping amongst the nettles and green shrubbery between them a shoeless man. The bins overflowed, and the towpath benches were providing respite for a few achy-limbed drinkers. I tilted my head as I passed under an old photo-worthy bridge, light reflections dancing across its bricked arch that framed two loved-up swans making heart shapes with their snake necks. On the cellulite-dimpled water, I could see stagnant sludge and puddles of white scum floating on the surface. My eyes, though, filtered out the litter, the oily swirls on the water, the chaotic towpath, and could see only the lushness of the trees, the colourful floating homes and the wildlife enjoying the water. At the next lock, the silent canal turned from calm to wild and loud, as water gushed through gates, forming a bubbly white urban waterfall.

This world seduced me. Perhaps it was because it felt like one of the few places where people looked up from their phones, where people forgot that they were busy. Perhaps I was subconsciously drawn to it because, despite the chaos, diesel-filled waters and shit, there was wildlife. Perhaps the allure was because waterways are where life happens. I couldn't say for sure. But what I did know was that the water's pull on me was strong, and I wanted to catch its current. Here, the speed was slower, the sky was wider. Here, it just felt right. For the first time since I'd lived in London, I felt like this was where I was meant to be.

I was drawn to the boats, heavy barges and narrowboats in all their hues lining the canal. They reminded me of a colourful old gypsy wagon I loved when I was younger. They offered the freedoms that other mobile homes, like yurts, tipis and tents, have always provided for nomads. I'd always been on the move, but perhaps I was meant to be moving more? Only in our most recent history have people settled and permanently stayed in one place. We travelled for hundreds of thousands of years. Perhaps the draw to these boats was a faint genetic memory from my nomadic ancestors itching to be remembered. Perhaps being on the move was in my blood, a deeply ingrained behaviour waiting to be rediscovered? I longed for a secure home of my own, an escape from greedy city landlords, a connection to nature and community. I craved something simpler, a window that looked out onto something more wild, something other than buildings, a life more than work, pubs and heart-breaking boys. Perhaps a boat was the answer?

I knew nothing about canals or canal life but, by the time I got back to my house-share, my mind was made up. I knew what I needed to do. If I was to survive in this dense, lonely, technology-obsessed, expensive city, if I was to have a home of my own which no one could take away from me, I would need to live on a boat.

It took me a day to find *Genesis*. I had always moved fast, jumped belly-in to the unknown, trusting my intuition. This gut feeling was too strong not to act on, so I followed my instincts. I had decided I needed to live on a boat, so that is what I would do. I spent the night searching online for boats, eyes bleary but determined to stay open as I scrolled through vessels for sale on my phone before bed. I shortlisted a few moored not too far away, in Surrey, and sent out a bundle of messages. I set my alarm for 7am and woke to a few replies, three saying that I could view that day. I noted down the boat names and directions on a piece of paper, instructions like: "Park at the Anchor pub and walk towards the bridge... five minutes' walk above the lock... cross over to the non-towpath side." I jumped into my little car and headed off in search of a boat. The first was pretty, traditional-looking, red and green with stained glass in the front doors. Inside there was a lot of carpet. The second was slick, glossy. There was a large TV on the wall and the views were blocked out with black blinds. The third, the third was her. I knew it in an instant. She was moored on a backwater of the Thames, in a place I had never heard of called Chertsey, near Weybridge and Shepperton. A beautiful narrowboat, navy blue, forty-five feet long. She sat pretty in the water, waiting for me, with her smiling owners standing at her bow. *Genesis* was written in swirly letters along the side. I had

11

read somewhere that renaming a boat brings bad luck unless all sorts of superstitious rituals are followed, like renaming only when the boat is out of the water, walking around the gunwales (the side edges of the boat) backwards three times and purging every record of the boat's previous name. There are tales of shipwrecks and curses after the change of a ship's name. And so, *Genesis* she would stay.

The owner, Emma, was once a lock keeper. As we sat on the front deck in the spring sunshine, she told me of how she also used to steer Dutch barges across the Channel from Holland. Sitting beside her was her partner Terry, whose ancestry was English Gypsy. They lived within the Showman community on a site nearby. He told me about their horse, their vintage caravan that was parked on the grass, how he dealt in antiques, how they owned this patch of land and permanent mooring. "We want to build a small off-grid eco home in France," Emma said. "That's why we need to sell the boat." I instantly liked them. I was drawn to people who moved, and felt an affinity with groups who were unattached. Not just because we had something in common, with our transient lifestyles, but because transitory homemakers, gypsies and travellers seemed to me to be more in tune with how humanity once lived. Despite often being deemed by many as untrustworthy and strange, and in the past even imprisoned for being vagrant, I admired travelling communities, with their tight tribes, family members close by, outdoor lifestyle and traditions that can stretch back for centuries.

"Let me show you inside," Emma said. She opened the front doors and we stepped into the living space, with a bookshelf and sofa. There was no central heating, just a wood-burning stove which I would need to learn how to use well if I was to survive the winters. The boat smelled freshly cleaned but with a comforting yet unfamiliar scent, which I would later discover is one that many narrowboats have; a blend of chimney smoke, the outdoors and engine diesel. Light streamed through the large windows on either side. Beyond the stove was the kitchen, small but perfect with a rail for hanging pots and pans, and cupboards for food. It had a gas hob and oven which ran off two heavy canisters stored in the gas locker in the front of the boat (the bow) outside. She explained they were stored outside in this separate chamber for safety; a gas leak inside the boat could lead to an explosion. Where *Genesis* was moored, she was hooked up to shoreline power, and so a washing machine and normal household fridge were plugged into the 240V plug sockets. But she would not be staying here. I had done a bit of investigation into permanent moorings. They were way outside my price range, so I would have to be a 'continuous cruiser', only allowed to moor up somewhere for two weeks before moving on and be 'bona fide navigating'. That meant I could not be connected to mains electricity. I would be entirely off-grid. It would be more like living in a car with a cigarette lighter socket to charge things like a phone with a USB cable, using power stored in the leisure batteries. There were 12V plugs so I would be able to use low energy things but the washing machine and fridge would have to go.

Further in was a small bathroom that you could just about turn around in. It had a little bath with a shower over it, a plastic Porta Potti loo, a sink, a window and a cupboard with a gas boiler inside to heat the water. In the wall of the corridor was a side hatch: two little hinged panelled doors which opened outwards and above them another door which lifted back onto the roof so you could look up to the sky. The bedroom was a cabin-type corridor with a small raised double bed and drawers beneath for clothes. At the stern (back) of the boat was the engine room with cupboards for paints, ropes, sandpaper and pots of grease, and shelves for waterproofs and boots. Emma showed me *Genesis'* heavy engine, hidden beneath a puzzle of wooden boards and steps. It had organs and arteries made up of filters, an alternator, electrical wires and rubber cabling. Emma started her up, and the complex network whirred and vibrated in front of me in a loud unique rhythm, all parts working together to pump blood made of diesel, oil, grease and coolant through her metal piping and cylinders. Her metallic anatomy would turn the propeller, giving momentum to tonnes of steel and giving charge to the domestic batteries that the internal electrics drew power from. Emma talked me through it.

"If the engine's cold, twist this and hold it for a few seconds to warm it up first. Water goes in there, oil in there. That's your starter battery. When you're running the engine, turn this and it'll charge your two leisure batteries there."

She kneeled down and pointed to a metal tray beneath the engine, in the lowest internal part of the boat's hull. "That's the engine bilge. It catches drops of water that can come in when the propeller turns. You can pump the water out into the canal with this bilge pump, but if it's oily from the engine, you'll need to mop it all up by hand. Nappies are good for that."

"Right, OK."

"When buying a boat, the most important thing you've got to look for is a good engine; make sure it's been regularly serviced and maintained. And a thick hull. It depends on the original build thickness, but generally ten millimetres is ideal, six to eight is really good, anything less than four or five you don't want to go there, it could soon need over-plating." I was concentrating hard, trying to remember everything she said.

She took me outside onto the stern of the boat and explained the tiller, a brass arm which moves the rudder beneath the water to steer the boat, and how I would need to check the propeller hadn't got tangled in plastic bags, by looking through a weed hatch.

"This button here is your horn; if you're going through any tunnels or don't think another boat has seen you coming, give that a blast. Flick this one to turn your front headlight on. Remember to turn it off as it will drain your batteries."

"What's that dial?" I asked.

"That's the battery isolator. Position one for when you start the engine, two when you're running the engine, three when the engine is off."

"OK." I had no knowledge of engines or electrics, but my brain switched into a new practical mode; I knew I would absolutely have to remember all of this.

We went back inside to the living area, and I took the space in. I put my arms out wide and could almost touch the sides. There was no room for bits and bobs, or clothes not regularly worn. Everything I owned would need to fit into this slim corridor. I thought of what I would need to throw out. I would have to quickly learn the importance of putting things away as soon as they were finished with. In this small space even breakfast would cause a tidal wave of mess. I would need to find a folding table to eat at, put up hooks for hanging cooking utensils and cups to free up workspace, and find tubs for bedding to stop it from smelling of diesel. I tried to imagine the days when most of a working narrowboat would have been taken up with cargo, with the boatman and his family living in about a quarter of the space that was here. Around 1840, canal boats had to start competing with the new railways, which could carry more goods and much faster. Boatmen's wages were slashed, and their families had to leave their homes ashore and squeeze into cramped cabins, babies sleeping on the shelf of an open cupboard. In comparison the amount of room in *Genesis* now was palatial.

I thanked Emma and Terry for showing me their boat, said goodbye and drove halfway down the dirt track before stopping, pulling up the handbrake and squealing with utter joy. She was my perfect home.

It happened quickly. I haggled the price down, but still only had half of what I needed in savings. A small amount of Googling showed that marine mortgages existed but could be tricky to get, with interest rates way higher than for house mortgages. To my amazement, a man who looked too young to work in a bank said yes to giving me a personal loan. I quickly signed the paperwork before anyone more senior looking said anything otherwise. *Genesis* was booked in to come out of the water for a full survey, and I drove down to meet the marine surveyor. "She's solid," he told me, after a few hours of measuring steel thicknesses with an ultrasound machine and marking up numbers on the hull with chalk, and inspecting the entire interior. You don't have to get a survey when buying a boat, but it's widely recommended you at least get the hull surveyed. Emma was there too, and we signed a bill of sale that she had written up in the boatyard. It was a simple one-page document. Hand-written on it were our names, the boat name and the agreed sale price. I transferred every penny I had into her bank account, leaving no savings for emergencies. There was no solicitor, no additional paperwork that needed filling out, and no guarantee that Emma wasn't going to disappear with all my money. I had discovered that buying a boat wasn't like buying a house. Solicitors were rarely involved and it was a simpler affair that required a lot of trust. Somehow, the following weekend, I was picking up my boat. She was mine. I'd done it. In a week. Now I just had to get her to London.

16

I can't say I had done a great deal of research into what would happen after I became the owner of a boat. The only person I knew, or half-knew, who lived on a narrowboat was Paul, an ex-squatter-turned-anarchist-barrister. Every day, he left his barefoot life behind him as he disembarked on to the towpath in an immaculate suit. "I want to know *all* of the bad things about living on a boat," I'd told him. He raised an eyebrow, then started to reel off a long list. "Living on a boat is like a part-time job," Paul said. "Everything takes ages. Things break and there's always stuff that needs doing. Then there's the lack of privacy, emptying your own toilet waste every few weeks, sleeping a foot away from a public towpath in a capital city. And the fact that you have to move the boat to a different place or neighbourhood every fourteen days, and be genuinely travelling otherwise your continuous cruiser licence won't be renewed." He sighed. "And winter. Winter is long."

I nodded, and listened to his warnings. But none of this bothered me. I knew I was doing it no matter what. Now I was faced with driving my new floating home at a maximum speed of 4mph, with absolutely no boating experience, from Chertsey in Surrey to Victoria Park in East London where I had decided I would moor for the first two weeks because it was close to where my house-share was. I had looked over a map of London's waterways and roughly memorised the route, trying to remember all the unfamiliar names of the different stretches of water – the Grand Union, the Paddington Arm, the Regent's Canal. These waterways were a living museum of historic bridges and locks. They were slow, watery motorways dug by gangs of navvies, who lost limbs and lives shifting and shovelling earth with wheelbarrows and dynamite. They cut the land with bare hands to make a channel, which is why the canal is often called 'the cut'. The journey, which I had to do in a single weekend because of work, would be forty-three miles, passing through twenty-six locks and take around nineteen hours. The only thing I knew about driving a boat was what I had learned from a man in a pub who had given me a crash course in boat handling, using a beer mat as the boat.

The first day of bringing *Genesis* into London was going to be mostly on the tidal Thames. Unlike calm canals with water levels controlled by man-made locks, this river's levels rise and fall so there was a tide I had to catch, a strong current to contend with. An anchor and long chain needed to be onboard at the ready for emergencies. I knew my auntie, (my dad's sister) and uncle were calm and practical and had experience sailing, so I asked them for their help with the first leg of my journey. Thankfully they said yes. They came, exactly on time, with teabags, milk and sandwiches. I couldn't have been more grateful, and envied my two cousins, as I often had, for having such steady, dependable parents. Christmas at their house in Reigate in Surrey was always one of my favourite days of the year. It was the annual re-gluing of my family, and I was always welcomed and looked after.

The weather was perfect as we set off. I tried to remember everything Emma the owner had told me as she handed the boat over to me. *Steer the tiller to the left, she goes right, steer the tiller to the right, she goes left.* I ran this over and over in my mind until, after an hour or so, steering started to become intuitive and demand less attention. I tried to learn how *Genesis* responded, where along the boat she pivoted from. Steering from the back meant thinking more about pushing the stern away from where I wanted to go rather than steering the bow towards it. I practised slowing down and speeding up a little using the throttle, a lever tucked inside the engine room. As I relaxed more into steering, I began to take in the scenery and could chat with my auntie and uncle who were being my extra pairs of eyes and manning the ropes.

We were on the Thames, wide and open. Having not ever cruised a narrowboat on a canal, the scale of the Thames didn't worry me as I had nothing to compare it to. We cruised through Teddington lock, the largest lock system on the Thames – a huge watertight chamber with gates at both ends to control the level of water and raise and lower boats between stretches of waterways. Locks are used to make rivers more easily navigable and allow straight canals to be built over un-level land rather than winding around obstacles. Teddington Lock was electric and manned by a lock keeper who asked to see my river licence, required if you are navigating a river. I had bought one from the Canal and River Trust, the charity which maintains much of the country's canals and rivers and issues licences for boats using the waterways, but with the speedy purchase of *Genesis* the paperwork I needed to show and my boat numberplate, which was meant to be displayed, hadn't yet come through the post. Luckily, he believed me, and let us pass. I steered past Twickenham, noticing how much bigger all the other boats were than *Genesis* and how wide the river was, and went under Richmond Bridge, the city's oldest surviving bridge across the Thames. The strong river ahead looked glorious.

My naivety to the dangers of what I was doing, the excitement of having just become the owner of a floating home of my own, the concentration needed in learning how to steer in a single day, the exhilaration of being outdoors cruising down a great flowing river made the whole thing anything but scary; it was completely and utterly brilliant. The bank was busy with people enjoying the sunshine. I passed Richmond Hill, famously painted by J.M.W. Turner, which would later become the only view in England protected by an Act of Parliament. We passed Eel Pie Island, where the man who invented the wind-up radio lived, and where The Stones, David Bowie, Eric Clapton and Pink Floyd played some of their first gigs. Then, a sharp turning before entering the lock at Brentford. Quickly I shifted from the fast-flowing Thames to a stiller, slimmer body of water, the Grand Union Canal. Compared to the open expansive river we had been travelling along, which had felt familiar and London-like, the entrance to this canal looked foreboding, unknown, unpopulated. Ahead of us awaited a few more locks before a seemingly endless flight of locks at Hanwell. It was then I realised I didn't have a windlass, the large metal L-shaped key needed to work manual locks. The owners of another narrowboat who I had got talking to in the last electric lock, called Richard and Eleni, pulled up behind *Genesis*. They luckily had a spare windlass, and we tackled the relentless watery flight together.

Evening drew in. We had been travelling on *Genesis* for nine hours, covered twenty-one miles and worked sixteen locks. My auntie and uncle had to go home, and they were unsettled and worried about the unfamiliar territory where they were leaving me: a deserted stretch of waterway in Southall, just past the brick boundary wall of the old Hanwell Asylum. I watched them walk up the towpath. I was now alone, on a small blue boat, on a deserted canal. There were no other boats around and something about that place felt uneasy. There were some trees disappearing into the night, an empty towpath, and not much else in sight. It dawned on me that even though I now had a home, that meant living alone, upon the unlit borders between crime-stricken London boroughs, upon London's waterways where dismembered limbs, dumped bodies and suitcases of cash were found. The reality began to hit that my daily walks home would now be along dark towpaths, the kinds of places where people are violently mugged, where sexual deviants in search of thrills linger, drug deals are made unnoticed under dark bridges, and strangers disappear. Along that stretch of canal was, I would later find out, where a woman two years younger than me was strangled a few months before. Her dumped body, floating face up, was found by a dog-walker on Christmas morning.

My first night onboard was sleepless, and filled with worry. *Will I die of carbon monoxide poisoning? Am I safe? How am I going to manage tomorrow? What did Emma tell me to remember? Don't run out of diesel. Don't run out of gas. Don't run out of water. Twist this stern gland to add grease to stop water dripping in. If there's an emergency, pull the red stop button.* My body ached, not used to pushing open lock after lock, and my mind was swimming with everything I had to remember. Everything I'd learned about how to steer a boat that day was slipping out of my memory like a dream. The adrenaline was wearing off, and tiredness was setting in. Unlike my previous home on land, where the sounds of trains, sirens, music and traffic would fill my bedroom and my sleep, here on the water it was quieter. I thought about how I now had no mains electricity, no savings left for emergencies and no address. But I had *Genesis*, my new micro-home, my slim, steel, floating abode. She was going to be everything I needed.

Finally, 7am came around, and as promised, my friend Holly arrived to help me bring my new home *home*, or at least to where I would start my journey and what would be the first home of many. I had to go to work the next day and so we needed to cruise the entire length of London non-stop, from west to east, before sunset. The journey was twenty-two miles long with ten locks to go through, travelling along the Grand Union Canal, Paddington Branch and two-hundred-year-old Regent's Canal. I had calculated it would take us around ten hours, if nothing went wrong. Holly had come armed with supplies of crisps. I untied and wound up the centre line, the rope attached to the middle of the boat. Ropes, a heavy boat, water, fingers and a captain with just one day's experience were an accident waiting to happen, so I tried to double-check everything.

"Can you push her off the bank, Hol?" I asked, thinking how strange it was to be giving a friend instructions.

"Yep," Holly said, smiling. She pushed *Genesis* away from the bank and hopped back on. I pushed the throttle forward to accelerate. We were away. Immediately my worries disappeared and concentration took over.

"Boat, another boat coming towards you, Danie," Holly said, already the perfect first mate and fully understanding how much I needed her help rather than just company. I had been keeping roughly to the middle of the canal where it was deeper, but now veered a little to the right, letting the boat pass on my left like Emma had told me to. As I travelled past moored boats I remembered a little late that I was meant to slow down so as not to cause a wake and rock floating homes or dislodge mooring pins. *Genesis* got close to the moored boats. I slowed down, but there was still momentum behind the tonnes of floating steel. Holly stuck her legs out ready to fend off.

"Just let her bump, Hol," I shouted, panicked and feeling a new sense of responsibility. "Just let her bump, please don't snap an ankle." *Genesis* didn't bump. No broken bones. Beneath bridges of iron, steel, waste pipes and brick we travelled on, me at the stern steering, Holly on the roof ready to help and in charge of ropes. I soaked up London from a whole different perspective. Through Kensal Rise, tree-lined Little Venice, past London Zoo with its Snowdon Aviary, a giant multi-sided pyramid made of poles and nets, home to some of the world's rarest birds. It felt almost foreign, far away and exotic, but these were London's watery edge-lands.

The first lock of the day lay ahead. Camden, where tens of thousands of tourists had flooded in for the weekend to rummage through market stalls and watch boats go by. I could see the lock was set in my favour, meaning the water level was the same as the level of water my boat was on – another boat must have just come through – so I inched *Genesis* in slowly. I showed Holly how to close the upper lock gates and open the sluice paddles to lower her down. She listened carefully, and got it. Holly and I had only drunk and danced together before (we had become friends whilst studying Broadcast Journalism at uni). Now we were shifting tonnes of steel, working together in a perfect team. The water inside the damp brick chamber of the lock slowly lowered. I noticed how everything was big, heavy, slowed down – the very opposite of the lightweight, effortless, tap-an-app-for-anything world I had been living in. Attention-grabbing messages and emails had all completely left my mind. Right now, all that mattered was draining a lock so that I could continue my journey, and it was a process that could not be hurried. Hundreds of gallons of water lowered inch by inch. *Genesis* banged a little as water flowed until eventually the level equalled with the water below. I bent my knees and budged one of the lock gates with my bum, trying to walk backwards, leaning my weight onto it to open it, but it wouldn't shift. Holly did the same on the other side. After a few heaves in rhythm, the gates eased open. We closed the sluices, untied *Genesis*, clambered down the tall metal ladder hugging the wall of the lock and made a small leap onto the roof. I lowered myself onto the stern to take the tiller. Onwards. Onwards through King's Cross, Angel, Haggerston, and Hackney, slowly ploughing through reflections of moored boats, trees and clouds in wobbled water. An unknown upside-down city. Above a brick wall on the towpath side, I could see a busy road and the tops of cars whizzing by, oblivious to this hidden parallel slow lane.

Finally, at the end of two long days of driving *Genesis*, we arrived at leafy Victoria Park. Holly was at the bow looking for a space where I could moor. "There, just behind that green boat, should fit in there?" she shouted, having spotted a gap in the row of boats. I slowed *Genesis* down. With her nose angled towards the moored bank, I turned the tiller to swing in her bottom at the last moment. The precision of my manoeuvre surprised me. I was already in tune with how *Genesis* moved. With a few revs in reverse gear, she came to a heavy stop. Holly hopped off with the centre line and pulled her in, and I got to work looping the front and back ropes through metal mooring rings to secure the boat. My head was swaying. I brought in the removable brass tiller so it wouldn't get nicked, twisted the stern gland and isolated the starter battery. That was my checklist done. My brain melted. A drink was called for. We couldn't have been more proud of ourselves.

After a wander to a pub on the edge of Victoria Park and a swift half, Holly had to go home. Exhausted, I went to where I had been living for one final night's sleep on land, and one final long shower, before moving my things, which I had already packed up into a few boxes and bags and left in the middle of the kitchen. Aboard there was no room or use for unnecessary stuff and things which used a lot of power, and so I had thrown out my hairdryer, speakers, fairy lights, electric food processor, blender, iron, hoover, high heels, TV, electric kettle, toaster. It didn't bother me getting rid of these trappings of modern life. I was used to throwing things out. I'd moved so many times before and I was in practical, getting-things-done mode. It was only afterwards that I would discover I didn't need or miss these things. I would soon realise that most of my clothes looked fine un-ironed, that after ten years of styling my hair with heat, it looked and felt much nicer left to dry completely naturally, that always wearing flat comfortable shoes made me feel agile and free, that not being able to put a TV on made me happier, that tea tasted better from a slow-to-boil whistling kettle.

After work the next day, I handed over my keys to the house-share, squeezed my belongings into my small car – soon to be handed over to a man who overheard me in a pub saying

24

I needed to sell it to afford a boat – and drove towards *Genesis*, parking as close as possible which was still a five-minute walk through the park and down the towpath. I carried my things into my new home, back and forth, then went back to get my bike, cycling it over to *Genesis* and lifting it onto the roof. I was in.

That night as the sun began to set, people from the neighbouring boats came to say hello to me. They seemed to be impressed by my two-day twenty-hour voyage to this canal, and to think *Genesis* was a good ship. Everyone was having supper together, and they invited me to join them. Hatches opened and jam jars of tea lights transformed the stretch of concrete towpath into a flickering dining room. Plates and chairs of all shapes, sizes and colours spilled onto the towpath, and dishes of food were passed around between mismatched glasses and cups of wine. The ease with which this big group of disparate people chatted and shared their food filled me with happiness. I noticed an openness and trust among these boaters. A young couple handed their blue-eyed baby to a circus performer and went for a moonlit row across the water in a little wooden boat. A moment to themselves. The baby boy, who already knew more about life on the water than me, picked and ate flowers from a roof-garden box. The evening was clear, and trees reflected on the still water. Wrapped in a stranger's blanket, I warmed my soul with a tipple of inky sloe gin and smiled to find myself suddenly, and without fuss, accepted into this new and eclectic community.

2

On my first morning I awoke in my new home with a shock that I was still in London. I couldn't hear traffic, just birdsong. My eyes flicked open as the first early riser rode down the towpath, reggae playing from his small speaker as he whizzed past on his bike. I glanced at my phone. *7am*, a little earlier than I'd usually wake. Just 6mm of metal separated me from the towpath – my new doorstep. The floor beneath me rocked a little. This was exciting. Soon, the steady stream of gadget- and lycra-clad morning joggers and dog-walkers gave way to huffing cyclists and commuters on foot, waging their unrelenting battle for space just inches from my face. I felt like I was outside and inside at the same time. I got up and went out onto the front deck.

"An orange juice please," one lady said to me, mistaking me for a floating shop as I poured myself a glass on my front deck in my pyjamas.

"Oh, I'm not actually selling juice, I live here, but here, you can have this glass, I'll pour myself another."

On the towpath, where horses once pulled narrowboats filled with cargo, people strolled and drank coffee, some watching me sort out my things and open boxes. I was all of a sudden a bit of a spectacle, the subject of strangers' curiosities. It was odd, but didn't bother me much. Instead of buildings, I could see trees. Victoria Park, then my favourite park in London, was now a few steps away from my front door. I had spent afternoons walking through its pretty flower gardens, around its boating lake, over the bridge to the Chinese pagoda, drinking coffee from the Pavilion café by the fountain, picnicking on the grass with friends beneath London plane trees planted to absorb the city's lung-choking air pollution. I had seen the boats tucked just behind the fence. Now, this was where I was living. But not for long. I had a home, but it wouldn't stay in the same location. Without a pricey permanent mooring, I would never stay in one place for more than two weeks. London's canals were filled with a shifting current of people, moving to a new place every fourteen days, covering a range of at least twenty miles in a year in order to keep their continuous cruiser licence.

I had lost track of time and suddenly remembered I needed to head to Soho for a voice-over job. I didn't want to leave. I hadn't finished unpacking but already felt entirely settled. I shoved on the first floaty skirt I could find and tied a silk scarf in my hair. Aware of how many eyes were on me and my home, I tried to leave for work as discreetly as I could, shutting the side hatch and closing the padlock quietly. I jumped off quickly and distanced myself from the boat, so no one would notice she was now empty and unguarded. I hauled my bike down from the roof and cycled along the towpath to the Underground station, to be reabsorbed into the city.

During those first two weeks when I was moored at Victoria Park, I came to realise that my life had now been divided in two. I was constantly transitioning between the water and the city, straddling two worlds: the almost rural village life of the waterways and then the high-paced, high-rise, rapidly changing city. The Tube was my airless and tempestuous time-travelling machine, transporting me from an age without electricity into the new world of ultimate modern convenience. I found myself living across a threshold, in a state of liminality, not truly belonging to one or the other. A diesel stain on my clothes, mud flecks on my skin or dirt beneath my nails would risk blowing my cover among clean-cut city types who I feared would judge my boat home and find my new life strange. Like the families who lived on workboats over a hundred years before, marginalised from those on land, I already felt different. I'd quickly discovered that, the moment the word 'boat' was mentioned, a stream of questions would follow. How much did you pay for it? How do you get post? How do you wash? Do you have a toilet? Do you have electricity?

"Oo, Danie, have you been on holiday? Someone's looking all bronzed. Where've you been? Somewhere with lots of mozzies?" a fashionable young producer asked when I turned up at one of the Soho studios where I worked to record a TV promo for a kids' show.

Crap. I thought I'd sprayed enough DEET last night and smoked enough roll-ups to repel the mosquitoes but they'd feasted on my hot bare limbs as I'd sat and watched the night come in with my floating neighbours. Now the itchy red lumps on my tanned skin were at risk of giving away my new outdoor and grubbier existence, which I feared this producer might find weird, or just not really get.

"No, just, outside, a lot. How are you?"

"Yeah good, busy, right, OK, this is the script, let's get a few lines for levels when you're ready. Cool. How's the volume in your headphones for you?"

A producer by day, radio presenter by night, he sat confidently on the sofa of the studio with a cup of coffee from the café next door in hand as he directed me. He was wearing a chequered cotton shirt, sleeves rolled up, with a white T-shirt underneath, jeans, suede shoes and large-framed glasses.

"Nice, nice. Let's get one more of those in the bag, then try a cooler read next, not too cool though, and with a little less energy."

He gave me the thumbs up through the glass of the studio once he was happy, I said bye and then walked quickly to the next even shinier recording studio, which was a few streets along, this time to voice an advert for a new music single and album.

"Couchman, how's tricks girl, what's been happening?" This next producer I'd worked with before. He was funny, had an Essex accent and wore bright white trainers. He dropped names of dance music DJs, club nights and gave me more direction than was needed.

"This is a pretty upbeat track, so a nice, bright and smiley, high-energy read. Shall we have a watch through first?"

He was flirty, fast and tiring. Once he'd got a read he was happy with, I raced from the studio, clipping my hair up into a messy high bun, using that sixth sense Londoners develop that enables you to dodge fast- and slow-moving bodies without looking up. I wanted to get back to the canal. But I had one more job to do.

At the next studio, a young, petite woman introduced herself to me. She was wearing a patterned blouse, tight ripped jeans and shiny shoes, and was doing her best to assert herself and not let her inexperience show. I could feel her stress as she rambled about last night's work cocktails, the next big things, how busy she was.

"Shall we get cracking?" I suggested. This time I was voicing an ad for a reality TV show. Each of my working days was as fragmented as the last, bouncing between different studios across five London boroughs, which made routine impossible. A nomadic life in a home which needed to be moved to a new place every fortnight wasn't going to make routine any easier, but I didn't think about that then. I embraced the variety and newness. And anyway, it was too late to go back now.

"OK, Danie, can you hear me alright? OK, cool. For this one I think come in a bit closer to the mic and drop a level in pitch, and, er, read without too much of a smile, maybe add in a little huskiness."

As she stood up to take another urgent phone call I thought about the night before on the canal. Candles, rugs, cushions, bikes and big bowls of food all scattered over the towpath. The smoke from the barbecue and fire pit made everyone's eyes tear and it was still caught up in my hair. The sound engineer gave me a friendly smile through the glass from behind his big desk of glowing buttons.

"That's the one. Er, OK, that was take three, um, OK, we can go on to the next version of the script, which is exactly the same except for one word in the, er, the second line."

All that was on my mind was getting home and exploring my new world. I found myself longing to disappear back to my watery edge-lands, to slip away like a fox or a bat. I hadn't chosen this career because I was desperate to work in TV. My job didn't fill me with a deep sense of purpose, but it had been a long journey to get here so I needed to make the most of it. After funding my way through university with whatever temporary jobs I could get, I worked for free for months as a TV and radio news reporter, enduring the wrath of story-hungry career addicts telling me to watch their illegally parked car while they attended a press conference, or to hide while they filmed the mourning mum of a gunned-down boy after being told to respect her privacy, or to lie on a sun-bed in my underwear for a set-up shot to a story on skin cancer. I grafted as a newsreader and reporter in a small radio station by the sea, working six days a week for the minimum wage, with my first bulletin at 6am. Finally I got my break and landed a job as a TV continuity writer and announcer in London. It was then that a voice-over agent signed me up and I began to get bookings.

If I'd been given careers guidance at college, perhaps I would have headed down another path instead and become an anthropologist, a documentary maker, a treehouse builder, a psychologist, or a storytelling poet. But I had somehow climbed a long way up this ladder and found myself working as a voice-over artist and TV writer. This career was not noble, or life-saving, it did not feed my soul. But I was giving it everything I had, fuelled by an unshakeable motivation and determination, a longing to be able to afford a home where I could raise a family.

My childhood hadn't been stable. After our nomadic years as a four, Dad left the army when I was eight so my younger brother Ben and I could stay in one school. He became a freelance commercial photographer, and we moved into a skinny brick Victorian house with a skinny garden and steep stairs. The house was in Reigate in Surrey, the town in the south-east of England where my aunties, uncles and cousins lived, on a street filled with kids who liked water fights. Mum filled the garden with roses, cut back the hedges and grew courgettes, sweet peas, raspberries, tomatoes, corn and herbs. Her garden was her solace. The house smelled of candles, and music would play from the radio in the kitchen. Ben and I spent summers running through bracken in the woods and park near our house, following streams. We'd play on the street with all the other children, or roll about with the numerous dogs that we looked after for pocket money when our neighbours went on holiday. We had two cats called Bill and Ted, a mad Staffy called

31

Dolly, a white rat called Betty, a guinea pig called GP, a rabbit called Peter and colourful fish. We'd draw patterns all over the street in coloured chalk, and decorate Bluebell, Mum's beat-up 2CV car, with poster paint. My friends and I would make up dance routines and plays in the garden and cast fairy spells in my room. And for a few years, each summer we went away on a holiday, the four of us. We stayed on a boat called Moon Beam on the Norfolk Broads, in a log cabin in Wales near the coast which had goats outside, in a B&B on the beach of the three-mile-long Channel Island of Alderney and in a caravan in France. We always stayed close to water.

Then, after Dad said goodbye from the bottom of the stairs when I was eleven, things changed. His affair left destruction and disruption in its wake. My beautiful, brown-eyed mum lost her colour. Mum had suffered from periods of depression since I was very young, but these episodes now became more frequent, especially in winter, and we slipped below the poverty line. Adamant that Ben and I would stay settled in our school, Mum did her best to ignore the increasing debts to avoid having to move again. She propped up the broken kitchen cupboards with tins of beans, got Ben and I on free school lunches and took extra shifts at the hospital where she worked as an auxiliary nurse. If Mum wasn't on a long early or late shift, she would be juggling housework or in bed resting or weeping. I missed her, I missed our carefree family life, but instead of being sad, I would be angry. I would shout and scream, storm out and slam doors. I didn't know what was going on, why everything was different. Mum's periods of sadness frustrated me, I wanted her to be strong. My child's mind didn't understand the overwhelming pressures she was under as a single working mum of two, how much her life as well as mine and my brother's had changed.

Later her spirit would be washed out further as she was forced into silence by her new Sun-reading, Stella-drinking boyfriend, who swooped in and began paying the mortgage that she could not afford by herself. His solid, brick-like body loomed over my small, butterfly-like mum. I nicknamed him 'the Wolf' and kept out of his way as much as possible. We didn't understand why Mum endured him, but she couldn't leave him. His control had drained her of self-esteem and confidence. He was an emotional and financial bully. She thought she'd be homeless and nothing without him. Going to work was her refuge. She would put on a 50p floaty skirt from the charity shop and her orange lipstick to hide the invisible wounds inflicted by his psychological battering. I knew when Mum was really low, when things were really bad, because she wouldn't have her orange lipstick on.

Ben and I would go to stay with Dad every other weekend. He'd bring us round to new girlfriends' houses, each with different rules and families to impress, people we didn't know to make birthday cards for, new kids to have to get along with. Dad was fun, creative, silly, but he had no routine, and would often lose his temper in frustration with Ben and me. As we grew older and things got worse at Mum's with the Wolf, Ben stayed at our Auntie's or with school friends. Eventually, Dad bought an ex-council flat so that Ben would have somewhere to live whilst at college. Dad would sometimes stay when he wasn't at his girlfriend's, but Ben mostly lived there alone. By this point I had left town for university, and during the holidays I would stay with my boyfriend's family or in a school friend's attic. The flat was forever in a state of disrepair and unfinished DIY projects, with no spare room for me. Inside were stripped and half-painted walls, which held no family memories. The floor was mostly bare and sometimes had holes through it, and the bedroom was filled with Dad's photography equipment. There was no dining table to share a meal around. The temperamental fridge in the kitchen would contain a few fancy pickles and cheeses, perhaps some fresh pasta, but was not stocked with enough for meals. If I came to visit for a night, I would sleep on the second-hand sofa-bed in the lounge. Dad would usually be busy with work or have something else on with friends, and sparks of emotion would ignite into arguments. I was becoming strong-willed and independent and found it hard to hold my tongue, especially when any angry words were aimed at Ben, three years younger than me. When heated rows would erupt I'd leave the flat sobbing, walking to I didn't know where, wishing I hadn't come. Sometimes I'd find a kerb to sit on, and wait until I was too tired, and then go back. Sometimes I'd try to think of where to run away to, who to run to.

Ben reacted to these difficult years of our childhood by learning to adapt and move on. He had the ability to fit into any group of people, and hold a conversation with anyone. Like a tortoise, he survived by carrying his home with him, and as soon as he had saved some money of his own he became travel-obsessed, back-packing to country after country. While I focused on work, relentlessly saving in the hope that I could one day afford a home, Ben coped by wandering the world. He journeyed through almost seventy countries on a shoestring. A true explorer, and completely resilient.

"I just saw a terrapin in the canal!" Holly said, brimming with excitement as she walked up to the front deck. With her delicate face framed elegantly by long dark hair and her leggy figure, she might appear too polished for my new unwashed boat world, but she was always pitching up to help at just the right time. After two weeks in Victoria Park, and two weeks in Mile End, today I needed to move *Genesis* to a new place to moor but I needed to fill up with water first. There was a tap on the towpath just a few boats down at the lock. I pulled *Genesis* closer to it, connected one end of my hose to the tap with a small bit of twisty plastic, and ran the other end into the boat's water tank, which sat beneath the front deck. This supply would have to last me until I next found a tap, whenever that would be. After almost an hour, we got on our way. I was planning on heading west along the Regent's and finding somewhere to moor near Broadway Market. I was surprised at how I already felt in tune with *Genesis*, her length, the sound of her engine.

"That looks like a nice spot there, Danie, will *Genesis* fit?" Holly said, turning her head towards me when talking so I could hear her over the engine. She was at the bow, scoping out where would be nice to have a garden for the next two weeks. I pulled up on a curved stretch of the canal on the towpath side opposite the old gas works of Broadway Market, which once supplied the gas to illuminate the city's streets, its position designed to make it easily reached by barges of coal coming from the docks. I moored *Genesis* next to a battleship-grey narrowboat which didn't seem to have a name. Aboard was Steve, a young saxophonist who I'd soon discover always looked the same whether he was drunk, high, or neither: glitter-dusted and topless. His boat was mostly empty except for a ramshackle collage of instruments tacked up on the walls: drums, a maraca, a guitar, a glockenspiel. He shared the boat with his friend Tim, who had squeezed a piano on board with him. In dirtied jeans, and with a hole in the neck of his T-shirt, Tim tinkered on the keys whilst Holly and I drank tea, listening from a large, comfy cushion on the floor, which must have doubled up as someone's bed. Later Tim shoved the upright piano onto the towpath, wheeling it along to play for a bob or two, singing old blues while Jazzy Steve blew the sax. Tim was halfway through building a chicken hutch on the roof of his boat, but he was soon to discover that protecting his clucking, feathered friends from cyclists and city dogs, eager to be off the lead for their brief moment of freedom, was too much of a task. The scratching of feet on the roof would be the final straw, and Tim put them up for fostering to another boater. Being moored next to these two, the next few weeks were to be filled with music.

My new addressless address was right in the middle of a thronging mini-world within the city – a glorious sensory overload. Just up a few steps from the towpath was Broadway Market where there were buskers playing Balkan music, people selling homemade cakes and cheese, an old pub where gangs of eighteenth-century thieves used to rob local tradespeople, all under the haze of barbecue smoke. Music drifted over from the many clashing sound systems of people partying in London Fields, a park at the north end of the market street that was once the last common grazing land for cattle and sheep on the way in to London. Days rolled into nights that rolled into days, and the towpath was fruitful with frivolous, impromptu adventures. I drank coffee on the kerb and listened to a busker plonking a double bass to a gypsy jazz beat, accompanied by a banjo and fiddle played by older gents in fabulous attire. I basked in the spring warmth, watching a woman sway a baby on her hip whilst she sang along to her husband playing the accordion. I had lived in Hackney for a year on land, but being on the waterside was different. Here, it was a summer-long festival, where everyone talked to everyone and anything could happen.

"Shall we give *Genesis* a wash?"

Holly decided my boat needed a good scrub. I'd been aboard just a few weeks but already a layer of London muck had coated *Genesis*' navy-blue and cream paint.

"Are you sure? You don't have to, I could clean her another time?" I asked her.

"That's OK, it'll be fun, won't take long. Have you got sponges?"

But before our sponges had even been dipped into the bucket of warm, soapy water up on the steel roof, long-haired, softly-spoken Matías who lived on the boat in front, came to say hello. Once a high-flying lawyer in Argentina, he'd left it all behind to make silver jewellery, selling it from a bench hung on the side of his long, black, narrow home. He brought treasure to the towpaths of London, like an old sea merchant hawking new spices and foreign riches from afar. Matías' conversation was slow, gentle and reassuring, and I felt safe knowing he was moored next door. Holly and I drank *mate* tea from his carved wooden gourd then went back to the task of scrubbing. But as we re-soaked and soaped the sponges, there came the word "sangría?" from the Spaniards who were double-moored alongside *Genesis*. They were standing on their roof, holding out a jug filled with red wine, lemonade and oranges. It was impossible to resist, and so the party that being moored at Broadway Market brought continued into the night.

The little red light on the control panel, next to the button for the horn and front light, wasn't going out like it usually did when I started the engine. There were many buttons, switches and sounds to get used to on the boat, but this little red light not going out made me panic. I thought back to how Emma had told me to watch out for this. "If the little red light doesn't go out when you run the engine, the..." *What did she say? Oh, the leisure batteries. It means they aren't being charged.*

I looked at the engine for a while, trying to spot if anything looked different to when Emma had shown me it whirring. By a stroke of luck, the couple who had given me their spare windlass on my first day – Richard and Eleni – happened to pass by on their way back to their boat and offered to take a look. "It looks like your alternator bracket has cracked." They were really turning into my boat guardian angels. I called a marine engineer who said it would be fixed when it was fixed, and ordered the part.. But with no solar panel yet to keep the batteries topped up, this meant no electricity. This also meant no shower, as the pump that pressured the water needed power. And so for ten days whilst moored at Broadway Market, my day-to-day existence became inconvenient but thrilling. I got around not being able to shower by carrying home big bottles of water and boiling a kettle for a flannel wash. Strangely I didn't mind one bit. It all felt like a weird holiday. The boat was already teaching me lessons of patience and slowing down that would prove invaluable in the months, and life, to come. Life was now harder, requiring more effort. But it felt right, like I was truly living, rather than just existing.

I was living alone but I didn't feel lonely. Jazzy Steve, Tim and their friends were always around when I got back from work, and different boat neighbours came and went. A couple younger than me who sanded their roof from morning till night and waved whenever I got home, their eyes visible above dust-covered decorator's masks. A TV editor who made me cry with laughter each time we spoke. A man about fifteen years older than me with long black dreads and the most loyal, well-behaved dog I'd ever met. A boy my age with a ginger beard who lived on a seafaring barge and worked as some kind of business consultant, and had just got a kitten. A smiley woman with curly hair whose partner played the fiddle. I chatted with them all. Everyone was wonderful, and I began to realise that I had joined a community of people who were never in the same place but nevertheless always looked out for each other. There was also a single burst of visits from land friends. They each came, enjoyed a cup of tea or glass of something on the deck in the sun, took photos. It was summer, and a novel day out for them, but after they'd come once or twice, their visits stopped. It wasn't their thing, and even though I was still in London, to them, having a constantly changing location that was rarely close to a tube station, I may as well have been living in the middle of nowhere. But this was now my world. I would lose touch with all but a couple of them.

It was urban along this stretch of the Regent's Canal, but even here in Zone 2, rather than sirens and cars I heard small birds singing from bushes, watched moorhens with their shiny black feathers and poster-paint red and yellow beaks pecking around the grass verges like little chickens (they seemed to prefer being on land more than the coots), prehistoric looking black birds which I learned are called cormorants fishing, fluffy ducklings following their mums and endless cute dogs strolling along the towpath. I saw swans flying heavily in the sky, necks outstretched, feet tucked beneath their large bodies, their wide white wings slowly beating the air. I would watch them come in to land. Their feet would run in mid-air and then, as they met their reflection, they skied across the water, disrupting the calm for just a moment. From large airborne gliders to elegant water creatures, they folded their wings back and paddled on, not caring about the seagulls circling and squabbling for stale bread.

When the engine was finally back up and running, I was on the move again. As I steered into the first lock, from Broadway Market en route to Angel, a long-haired traveller from New Zealand spotted me and asked if I needed a hand. I was grateful for the extra help. When we finally moored up, we kissed in the dark and fed swans from the front deck. He was like a gentle wild creature from nowhere. His eyes were green and everything felt as it should. He ended up staying aboard for a week before he flew home. We walked barefoot together along the canals, swam and climbed trees, made love, cooked, and held hands. He told me I was a wonderful person, that he felt privileged to have met me. He wasn't like the other boys. In the few years I had been living in London I had been pursued by and ended up on dates with boys I wished I'd never met: a posh boy who power-dressed, a persistent radio presenter who turned out to be married, a film director who only wanted to spend time in the bedroom, a history teacher too tired to meet up, a lawyer who didn't believe in monogamy, a musician too free-spirited for a relationship, and a chef who I discovered had a pregnant girlfriend. This boy was who he was, he did not have an ego or hidden agenda. He was kind. I was glad to have met him. I felt closer to the ground and the sky with him.

"I can do your laundry! My mate lives in a flat round the corner, he's got a washing machine," a scraggly Captain Jack Sparrow-looking bloke called to me, spotting me heaving a heavy bag of dirty clothes out of my boat. I had only done a couple of laundry runs so far, and didn't particularly enjoy cycling with a large rucksack filled with laundry on my back or in a trailer to a random, usually fairly empty launderette and watching laundry whoosh and whirl around for an hour or so.

I was now moored in Angel with its skinny, busy towpath, canal-side gastro pubs and trendy cafés, trip boats, locks where local workers congregated to eat their lunch, and, a colony of exotic eight-foot-long Aesculapian snakes were breeding beneath the water's surface, according to the paper. Thirty had been spotted, but no one knew where they had come from. Perhaps their ancestors escaped from London Zoo.

"Really? That would save me a mission," I replied, apprehensive but slightly relieved. I had met him the day before as he stood, bare-chested and skinny, plugging up a hole on his white fibreglass cruiser with gaffer tape. He'd bought his small, light boat cheap because it had sunk, he'd proudly explained. How it had sunk he wasn't sure. It could've been from rainwater getting in, too much weight, or the bilge pump siphoning water back into the boat rather than emptying it out. He said someone tried to re-float it with petrol-powered pumps, but that didn't work, so ropes were tied to two boats on either side and it was slowly winched up to the surface. The missing windows were draped with colourful fabric, and unlike *Genesis'* sides of steel, its thin fibreglass frame looked delicate and easy to crack. These speedier, lighter types of craft, sometimes affectionately nicknamed 'Tupperwares' or 'yoghurt pots' by boaters, were the canal's equivalent to a nippy modern caravan. Narrowboats were more like the waterways' version of the far slower, more traditional gypsy wagon designed to move at the pace of a walking horse.

Laundry was now a whole new inconvenient exercise in logistics. When entire families lived on the old working boats, clothes were washed in a tin tub with canal water and hung out on a washing line strung up over the boat. Nowadays, with enough solar panels you could power a washing machine on board, but one washing cycle would almost drain my entire water tank. And so, what used to be a simple click of a button had turned into hours of wandering down strange backstreets, searching for launderettes that seemed to elude Google Maps and be trapped in a time warp.

At weekends, my least favourite launderette doubled as a buzzing clothing pop-up shop where couples in vintage would rummage through the racks of fabrics hung on the graffiti-covered, club-night- and yoga-poster-clad walls. But during the week, the mostly unsupervised space became a refuge for anyone with nowhere much else to go. During one of my visits, a couple had settled themselves in the corner to have an argument, spitting a confusion of half-finished sentences at each other while smoking crack. Nearby, a hunched lady scuffled in behind me wearing a stained dressing gown and not much else.

"FAAAG?" she pleaded, gesturing a smoking action with empty fingers.

"Sorry, I don't have any," I said, adjusting my weight to cope with the heavy bag of laundry. I turned my jean pockets out in hope of enough change for the machines. I wasn't in a contactless-card world now. I didn't have enough, and so risked leaving my dirty laundry on top of the washers and ran across to the bookies to change up a note and race back. The coins were swallowed by the machine, again. Another note scribbled to let the invisible launderette staff know. A piece of A4 paper taped to the front window advertised "Service Wash". There was no sign of anyone working there, and last time I paid the extra for someone else to do the washing and drying, a stranger's leggings came home with me, and a couple of my pairs of pants ended up in someone else's drawer.

My Jack-Sparrow-cum-Artful-Dodger neighbour reassured me. "Course, sister, it's no problem at all. I'm going there later," he said, heaving my giant, diesel-infused wash bag onto his front deck. I didn't see this bag again for a while. Before he got to his friend's flat he stopped on a boat for a drink, leaving my bag aboard, which then sailed away to the wild west of London. I strangely didn't mind too much; the randomness I'd already witnessed on the canal meant it almost didn't come as a surprise. And I liked this guy, there was something about him that meant I couldn't be mad at him. He had mislaid most of my clothes, but he had tried to help me. And, he was a boater. After a series of messages I managed to get my bag of unwashed laundry loaded onto someone else's boat which was cruising eastwards to Angel, and picked it up.

Sparrow was an entrepreneur of sorts. He would give impromptu tours of the Regent's Canal on his small cruiser to groups of tipsy hip young twenty-somethings he'd just met. He'd take them along the canal that had been lined with brick warehouses and factories as the city grew. It was changing still. The buildings along it were once built with small or no windows on the canal-side to avoid the vista of horse-drawn barges carrying up to thirty tonnes of dirty cargo, chemicals, dynamite and manure. Now, it had become a desirable location to live, and waterside new-builds with balconies and floor-to-ceiling windows to take in the view were springing up everywhere, smoothing out the canal's rugged textures with cold glass, flat fronts and characterless uniformity: architecture that benefitted from being next to the canal, promising waterside views, but yet giving nothing back to it. A one-sided discourse.

Sparrow would take his unofficial tour boat through the near kilometre-long historic Islington tunnel, explaining how without a towpath for the horses to pull the boats, boaters would 'leg' through, lying on their backs on the roof of the boat and walking their feet along the roof of the tunnel. Later on, a steam tug attached to a continuous chain running the length of the tunnel was used to tow barges through. Sparrow's loud outboard engine would roar as he tied up to the back of *Genesis* late at night to collect his tourists. My boat would rock as he and his punters walked across my stern to hop aboard his boat for a cruise into the blackness of the long towpath-less tunnel which seemed to go on forever. You're not meant to run your engine between the hours of 8pm and 8am, unless you're navigating, but it was the only way he was managing to pull in a bit of cash, so I turned a blind eye and a deaf ear. The other floating neighbours soon had enough of Sparrow, his late-night cruises and long, ridiculous stories, but I warmed to him. He was alive, full-on, always smiling, and always trying to make his life work. Often I couldn't tell if he was high, drunk, excited or all three. I got into the habit of putting any leftover dinner in a Tupperware box for him and leaving it on his boat.

Sparrow spent his days with his friend Frank, an older, rounder, rosy-cheeked fellow who enjoyed fishing for tiddly fish in the canal. One time he told me he was "keeping his head down". From who, or what, he didn't say. I didn't ask. For my twenty-sixth birthday, this Oliver Twist pair bought me a bottle of bubbles and sang to me from the towpath.

" 'Appy birthday, Sis," Sparrow beamed as he handed me a card filled with heartfelt birthday wishes from boaters and local shop owners, most of whom I'd never met. The jazzy boys were there too. Steve brought his sax and played from my front deck. His friend and his friend's brother came too, a few boaters I'd recently met, and Holly. Sprawled out on the boat roof, front deck and towpath we drank and smoked, talked to swans and danced. *Genesis* swallowed up ten people that night. Every inch of her insides contained a sleeping body. One head rested by the rusted robot-like cooker in the dark green tiled kitchen, another snored below the open side hatch. Three squeezed into the small cabin bedroom and three more slept in the main galley in and around the makeshift sofa-bed. I found myself squashed in the two-foot-wide corridor with a shaggy-haired young photographer and a white Staffy who looked a bit like a pig with dark spots on her belly. I was looking after her for Sparrow. He'd promised his friend he would take care of her, but then something else came up. In the morning, dishevelled and barefoot, we piled out onto the towpath and I made tea, toast and a big pot of scrambled eggs. The dog wouldn't leave my side.

A few months on I learned through floating river whispers that Frank had had a big night and had dropped dead. I heard that the boat Frank was found on was set alight in his honour, as a caravan would be in ancient traveller and Romany gypsy tradition. I imagined how the boat would have blistered into the night, flames roaring and lashing through windows, thick smoke lurching upwards, until all that was left was a semi-sunken charred carcass. I shed a tear for him, and wondered what happened to his dog, who was always by his side. The next time I saw Sparrow he was begging on a busy street in Tottenham, homeless once more.

I sat on the front deck of *Genesis* smoking a roll-up. The evening air was balmy. As I watched cigarette smoke swirl into the night's sky, I saw a dark-haired man casually paddleboard past me. He glided through the water before jumping onto the stern of his green boat, called *Madame George*, a few boats up. I decided to say hello. Barefoot, I walked back out on to the towpath, bringing with me a pot of chai, a couple of cups dangling from my fingers.

"Knock knock, just your neighbour," I said from the towpath. This boat looked worn, the paint job had scratches and faded patches where the forest green had lost its shine. The wooden deck was weathered and in need of sanding and varnishing. Plants outside were green and mostly lush, with just some dried tips.

"Hi, come on in," a voice replied. He introduced himself as Sam, and carried on doing what appeared to be stretching exercises. He rolled his shoulders back and, with an upright posture, casually lunged, uber comfortable but still picture-poised. He was wearing well-fitted blue jeans and a black T-shirt and, seemingly unfussed as to whether I was there or not, he focused more on stretching. He had a slight nonchalance, which weirdly made me want to grab his attention more. Inside, the boat was homely and easy to move around in, being ten-foot wide rather than six foot ten. The interior was homely and functional. There were signs of long weekends away and of more fun things to be doing than the washing up straight away.

"Have a look around if you like. It's always nice having a snoop around someone else's boat!" he said. On the sofa there were thick knitted blankets, and a cafetière of cold coffee sat on the side, wrapped in a multicoloured woollen jacket.

"Love your coffee pot's jazzy jumper," I told him.

"My mum crocheted it," he replied proudly, rubbing his thick, neatly trimmed beard. Kitesurfing gear poked out from behind his sofa alongside climbing harnesses and ropes. Hanging on a hook were goggles that I predicted had seen many a wild swim.

"Do you climb?" I asked him.

"When I get the chance. There's a couple of good indoor climbing walls nearby, I'm planning on a big climbing trip in Spain soon actually. Shall we have some of that tea then?"

Sam, who was a neurologist, told me about his adventures. Once he spent a month on a desert island with a bunch of guys, having to kill a crocodile to survive. His energy was intoxicating. After two years on inland waterways, he was still full of enthusiasm for river life, and blessed with the ability to completely ignore the curious eyes of people who strolled past the boat's windows. He would cycle each day from his boat to the hospital where he worked, then come home and let the canal wash away the day. I immediately saw in Sam someone who could become a friend, and when a couple of days later he went floating off in the other direction, I hoped our paths would cross again.

3

"So, what's the toilet situation?" It continued to surprise me how many strangers would ask what I had for a toilet on the boat. I usually explained, with hollow enthusiasm that dwindled with each recurrence, that there were two types: pump-out loos, which needed sucking out, and Elsan cassette loos, or Porta Pottis, which you'd add chemical toilet fluids to. On *Genesis* I had a Porta Potti, where all the waste went into a portable box, rather than into a big tank built into the boat from where it could be sucked out. This meant that, when it was time to empty the loo, you had to take the box to an Elsan disposal point by hand. When the loo was full, it was heavy, too heavy for me to lift for more than a few seconds. I would drag it from the bathroom across the kitchen floor, crap sloshing within, to the front door, heave it onto the towpath, ignoring all eye contact with passers-by, and lift it into my bike trailer. I would then cycle it along the skinny towpath, thighs burning as I pulled the heavy load over bridges, to the nearest Elsan disposal point, a big stainless-steel flushing loo that was often blocked and overflowing, forcing you to step through, breathe in and de-clog raw sewage. These smelly holes which you emptied your toilet into were for boaters' use only, and often behind a locked gate which could only be opened with a waterways key. If you put enough blue toilet fluid into your waste tank – a strong-smelling anti-bacterial liquid that helps break down the shit and toilet paper, and masks the smell – then the waste flowed out quickly when it came to emptying the holding tank, meaning the job was over and done with in a few minutes. However, it wasn't always that simple.

Elsan loos can quickly get full, especially if you have visitors. Once, not long after moving on to *Genesis* when I was moored in Haggerston, I got stuck one evening. The toilet was full to the brim and needed emptying, but the nearest place to empty it was out of order and I was booked solid with voice-overs in Soho the following day. I was too tired to do an hour round cycle trip with it to empty it somewhere else, so I had to think of another solution. I put the loo in my bike trailer and started walking, pulling it behind me, desperately trying to work out a plan. I spotted an open door on the towpath, a fancy office block, with a decorator in his white overalls, paint brush in hand, working late.

"Hey, don't suppose there's a toilet inside there I could use at all?" I said, without thinking.

"Er, yeah love, it's just up the stairs," he said, pointing up.

"Ah, thanks very much."

With my heavy, full toilet in a big Ikea bag, I struggled up the stairs, trying to make carrying something I could barely lift look effortless. It was one of the many moments where necessity and desperation unlocked a level of strength and resourcefulness I didn't know I had. I headed past the decorator and his pots of brilliant white paint, realising I hadn't thought this through. The tiny toilet cubicle was spotless. Freshly painted, and probably never used. *What am I doing?!* But it was too late now. I couldn't think of any other solution. If I could just empty my two weeks' worth of toilet waste here and now, I could go home and go to bed. So, I began emptying it, as carefully as possible. The waste splattered up on the walls and floor, pouring out into the loo quicker than I could flush it away. The small windowless cubicle stank so much I gagged. I did my best to clean up, thinking to myself that this must be as shitty as things get when it comes to toilets on boats. I left as quickly as possible.

"Thanks, see ya," I said as I left the building, avoiding looking the decorator in the eye, feeling extremely guilty for what I had done but also delighted that my toilet was now empty. I soon bought a second additional Porta Potti cassette to use when one got full, to avoid ever having to do that again.

My body jerked into consciousness, as I woke in the night to a tap tap tapping on the side of my boat. I was alone and the noise pricked each millimetre of my skin, and froze me into absolute breathless silence to try and hear what it was. There was only 6mm between us. The humanlike tapping then began sounding more like animal clattering, and I allowed myself to take a breath. *Perhaps it's just a swan and its signets pecking off weeds from the side of the boat*, I thought, in an attempt to reassure myself that I was safe. I knew that there was a luminous pea-green layer of water-loving duck weed carpeting the cut. Perhaps it was a swan. Or perhaps it was the man that police divers were searching for earlier. After a chase, a man had jumped into the water, but not resurfaced. Perhaps drowned, perhaps now tap tap tapping at my boat. Or perhaps the sound was from a canal monster, the water-wyrm of English folklore. Maybe it was a Scottish Shellycoat down to haunt these waters, its coat of shells clattering outside. Or a Nixe tapping at my door, a river mermaid lurking beneath the surface who'd made it across the water from Germany. Maybe it looked like my old plastic mermaid doll whose tail changed colour under the bubbly water of the bedtime bath sea. Or perhaps it was a croc. Boaters had reported sightings of a goose vanishing straight into these depths in an instant, and the rumour was that it could be a huge pike, or even a former pet alligator. Or perhaps it was the canal itself that was knocking, deadly with a greedy appetite begging for more. I wasn't brave enough to go outside. I didn't want to find out.

"Why don't you have a dog yet?" my brother Ben asked me. "You have your own place now." Ben was just back from a back-packing trip through Japan, China, Mongolia and Russia. We were sitting in a canal-side beer garden in Hackney Wick. The first autumn had arrived. The light brown curls on Ben's head were longer since we last saw each other and his stubble had grown into a beard. We didn't see each other that much, and if we did it was often in some crisis situation to do with our mum or at Christmas when there'd be lots of people, so I was enjoying this rare chance to have a relaxed chat with my brother. He might be younger than me but he felt like my protector. He was my solution finder, the wise voice at the end of the phone who wouldn't tell anyone what I'd said, the friend I'd had the longest.

Why don't I have a dog? I wondered. He was right. Before now, any rental property I'd lived in hadn't allowed pets. But I now had my own home. What was stopping me? I had always loved dogs. When we were young, Mum would look after people's dogs when they went on holiday, so our garden was regularly filled with multiple hounds which Ben and I played with and took out for walks with our friends. Looking after the white Staffy for Sparrow had reminded me how happy dogs made me; I loved the responsibility of looking after her and the companionship she gave me.

A few days later, I went down to Battersea Dogs & Cats

Home. Through metal bars, hundreds of dogs stared up at me with sad eyes, begging to be picked. Whichever one went home with me would need to be able to adapt to a constantly changing home, with a public back garden filled with other dogs, people and kids. I got a good feeling about one of them, a small female staffy. She had a slightly strange face and spark. But I was told she didn't like other dogs or cyclists, and I left feeling down and dogless. My heart was set on having a dog; I didn't care when other people tried to put me off, saying it was a big commitment. I wanted the responsibility, that special bond, a watchdog, a reason to get outdoors even more.

Then, in Angel a few days later, a beautiful hound with curly dark red fur caught my attention. He was standing calmly while his owner ordered a coffee from a little van. There was something about this dog. I found out it was a Cocker Spaniel/ Poodle mix – a breed known to be people-loving, other-dog-loving, and generally life-loving bundles of energy, and the perfect size for a boat.

"His parents have just had another litter," his owner told me. The same day, before I knew it, I was on the train to meet them on a big farm in rural Colchester in Essex to pick up a little bundle of white-and-roan curls.

It wasn't the best time for me to adopt a needy new family member. I had a new boat to handle, no one to help me with training or twice daily walks, no fixed address to order heavy bags of dog food to. Just as with the buying of *Genesis*, I didn't think about it too hard, even though my first winter on board, with all its unknown difficulties, was rapidly approaching. I just went with it, following my instinct that it would be good to have a companion on board, particularly one that could bark at strangers in the night.

Inquisitive and unfazed by his first train journey, my pup wiggled around, enjoying the squeals and strokes from other passengers, and then falling asleep as I watched the world whizz past the carriage window. I looked down at his eyes, small green-and-amber explosions, framed with long orange eyelashes, and realised, *I'm responsible for you, your entire being. You now depend on me to keep you safe and happy.* The feeling of joy I felt was indescribable. He was my dog, and my love for him was already unbreakable.

At London Fields station we switched train travel for a walk through the park. That year an urban meadow had been planted and we wandered through wildflowers, the nameless puppy up to his eyes in oxeye daisies, pink corncockle and poppies. The puppy dashed about in chase of an invading grey squirrel, then remembered he was looking for more dirty water, then noticed there were more birds to scare and more people to greet. A gaggle of high-pitched girls celebrating a thirteenth birthday mobbed him, passing him back and forth.

"Can I hold him now?" they each begged through ecstatic smiles, over and over. "Of course! Here you go." He was the party highlight. For the rest of our journey he played with other dogs for the first time and confidently trotted in every direction down through busy Broadway Market with its overflowing pubs and bearded bodies on curbs. Finally, we went down the steps onto the towpath, and boarded *Genesis* – his new home. My new shipmate immediately made himself comfy, snuggling up in the dog bed I had bought next to the yet-to-be-lit wood-burning stove. He and I were instantly bonded. With him, I felt, nothing was going to be impossible.

The puppy with no name became known as Mango, and he turned my boat into a public petting zoo. Even when I was sitting on the front deck, I would often find someone leaning across my shoulder to stroke him. Passing girls cooed to him in Spanish, toddlers squealed for joy at his wiggly bum and helicopter tail, and teenage boys greeted him like one of their crew: "Nice boat, brother." My walks became different too. With Mango I began to explore pockets of green close to where I was moored on the Regent's Canal: Shoreditch Park, Haggerston Park, London Fields, Victoria Park. London is the greenest city and the largest urban forest in the world, with eight million trees, but I was only now discovering it all.

Training was all encompassing. At puppy training classes in Haggerston, Mango and I would stand in a circle of puppies, of every size, colour and fluffiness. One flopped out flat, nonplussed, while another weed on the floor out of pure excitement, much to the embarrassment of its owner. One puppy barked wildly, and another sat perfectly, bow on her head. Mango was always desperate to say hello to everyone. As well as classes, I watched all the dog training YouTube videos, and read all of the dog training books.

He was – he is – the most energetic dog I've ever known. Even after hours of adventuring, he struggled to sit still. Training him was one of my biggest achievements, and a constant effort. But training would not be the only challenge we faced. The majority of London food stores, I discovered, are not dog friendly. Food shopping became tricky. When Mango was small, and before I'd worked out a routine to leave him at home for a short time, I'd sometimes go days without having enough food in the cupboard.

Once, when I'd exhausted the menu of meals possible to make out of what was left in the back of the cupboard, I decided to trust a man selling the *Big Issue* outside a supermarket with looking after Mango.

"Would you mind at all just looking after my puppy for me

while I quickly pop into the shop?"

"No problem, darling, love dogs, me. Used to have a Staff. Hello little one, hello mate. A boy is he?"

"Yes, he's called Mango. Thank you."

I rushed inside to do a sweep of food, popping my head out of the door every couple of minutes to check he was still there – which thank god he was, happily licking the man's face. When I went to pick him up, laden down with shopping, the man was letting him jump up all over him. I thanked him.

"Not a problem, love, not a problem. They know who likes dogs and who don't."

Mango and I both ate well that night.

I didn't quite realise how much energy I was consuming building my new life until the day I took a bath. I had been continuously cruising for five months, and been the single working mum of puppy Mango for six weeks. That week I had steered *Genesis* through gentrified Haggerston and Hoxton until there was a gap, just near where the Kingsland Road – built by the Romans – crosses the Regent's Canal: a previously disused canal-side space, now turned prime real estate. I moored up on a straight stretch beside a trendy café/gallery space, just downstream from a community-based boat club for children, nestled amongst old social housing estates and expensive gleaming new-builds. One of the new fancy canal-side flats, it turned out, was home to a friend of an uncle. My uncle mentioned I was moored nearby, and the friend came to knock on the boat one day.

"You're welcome to use my washing machine and bathroom any time you like while you're here, for a week whilst I'm away," he told me, mid-run and top to toe in lycra, handing me his spare keys. I'd never met him before, but I decided to take him up on his offer. It'd been a few months since I'd been in a house, or had a proper long wash.

I stepped out of my boat and walked towards the flat. A guy in army camouflage was chopping up pallets and hammering them together on the towpath. Next to him were two makeshift tents resting on top of inflatable dinghies, tied up to the bank. They provided him with a fragile shelter from the elements and a place to rest. He shared the same postcode as the surrounding multi-million-pound homes just metres away. He was savvy and resourceful, and I admired his inventiveness in creating a mini, mortgage-free shelter. The simple act of moving a tent from land onto the water meant he'd escaped being moved on by police. He was now the problem of the charity that looks after the waterways, and I hoped they would have more important things to do than turf out a person on an inflatable motor-less craft trying desperately to get by. I dodged a speeding bike, used the electric key fob on the gate, and stepped into the sleek apartment lobby. As I entered the lift I was taken aback by my wide-eyed, shaggy reflection. I hadn't seen my full body, brightly lit, in a while. The key to the apartment turned smoothly. I locked the door behind me and took in my new surroundings.

The sudden sense of privacy, calm and security was overwhelming. Here, in this flat, no one was going to come in at a moment's notice just to make their leisurely stroll along the canal more exciting. No strangers were going to be at the window, a foot or two away. I had the burning urge to spin and move around, to fill the space. Things were further than a metre away from me. Unused nooks and inefficient crannies looked wasted. The bathroom was so clean; a paradise, a spa, a sanctuary. I turned the taps in the bath, and watched it fill up to the top. A dull sense of unease readjusted to contentment as I realised that the water wasn't going to run out. Slowly I took off my layers of boat-smelling clothes. In the clean mirror

I looked at my olivey skin, darker tan on my bare back, which has always browned more ever since it burnt when I was nine. I noticed the mole to the side of my lip, my small boobs and waist, my maternal hips. I looked into my own eyes, large, green and brown. I studied my nose, small, a little wide, my ears unsymmetrical, one neat, one pinged out. Then, as I lowered my body into the hot water, unexpected tears fell.

Keeping up with my career and maintaining a moving, off-grid home alone had been quietly taking its toll. I hadn't had a moment to breathe, to think, to recharge. Here, lying in the bath in the home of a man I didn't know, I was safe to stop. Until that bath I hadn't had a moment for any restoration, there was nowhere on land I could take a break. My brave face was allowed to crack. Ignored feelings of being overwhelmed could now come to the surface. I could come to terms with the magnitude of what I'd undertaken, what my life and home now was; unpredictable, challenging, chaotic, wonderful, wild. My body looked different. Bruised and scraped legs from moving the boat, arms and stomach more muscular. I indulged in a slow soak rather than the usual every-other-day quick splash so as to not use up the limited water. After a while, I got out and put my clothes in this man's washing machine. It struck me how little effort this took. I was using an appliance without thinking about amps, or whether or not I needed to go outside and run the engine to power it. I wasn't in a strange launderette, finding the right change, trying to ignore all the odd goings on around me. All I had to do was close the washing machine door, and press a button. Just press a button.

My laundry smelled of diesel. I spritzed myself in frankincense, then, wrapped in a perfectly white towel, I sat on his sofa, staring out of the full-length window looking down onto the Regent's Canal. It was strange to see the canal from above, from this different perspective. As I watched life go on down below, people walking, boats going by, I knew that, despite the comfort of this stranger's sanctuary, I belonged down there. I stayed sitting there for just a little while longer, recharging, until I was ready to return to the water.

4

Autumn had fallen. It was rusty-red and tasted of root vegetable stew. As I steered my clinking steel boat towards the Islington tunnel on my way to King's Cross, I noticed that the air had changed. It was damper, cooler than the months before. The gustier days made it harder to cruise and at night winds shook and rattled my home, ropes creaking as *Genesis* jostled against neighbouring boats. The summer haze of towpath shenanigans was gone and the sun was mellower. Along the towpath were clusters of rosehips and blackberries, and my bare summered skin was getting paler beneath warm layers. I heaved open a groaning lock. Above me the barer branches of the trees began to reveal an even wider sky. Fallen curled leaves lay on the bow of *Genesis*. Next year, I would know that these blustery autumn days needed to be savoured, that the hardest months were soon to arrive and that I needed to be ready. But now, with each day so filled with new adventures and challenges, I did not pause to think about what was ahead. I felt the chill in the boat, but didn't do anything about it, I just wore more clothes.

Into the tunnel. I honked the horn long and loud, flicked the switch of the front light on and cruised *Genesis* into its dark mouth. I was surprised by how daunting I found it. I had steered through it just once, months before on the second long day of bringing *Genesis* into London, when in a daze of adrenaline and tiredness. Now I was far more aware of what could go wrong. Lacy cobwebs caught my face from somewhere in the dank darkness. I focused on the little circle of light ahead, keeping the tiller centred. *I must be halfway by now*, I thought, looking over my shoulder. *Shit*. I began veering too much to the left, then back to the right as I tried to straighten up. As I just about managed to avoid crashing into the walls, I began to see the light at the end of the tunnel, slowly getting bigger. Darkness transformed into bright light, and with my eyes adjusting, I slowly carried on at under 4mph in search of a spot to moor up. I tied up close to the tunnel. Home was now near the *Guardian* and *Observer* offices, near King's Cross and St Pancras Stations, where the Eurostar speeds to Paris (the sounds of station announcements can be heard from inside boats), Granary Square, and Central Saint Martins Art School, a former warehouse built in 1852 where barges would unload.

I didn't feel entirely comfortable in the place I found to moor up, not least because the weed-smoking guys on a boat nearby had already muttered dirty nothings to me as I'd tied *Genesis'* ropes to the bank. Luckily I soon found a friend.

"Do you want some eggy bread?" a voice asked me. I turned to see a young Buffy the Vampire Slayer lookalike dressed all in tight black velvet, with a blunt bob and fringe, slim and busty.

"I'd love some," I replied, hopping across the boat bows to my new neighbour's vessel.

She introduced herself as Jo. She was a 20-year-old Camden kid, magazine-cover ready with a bicycle tattoo on her wrist. She was beautifully barefaced but for a flick of black eyeliner, and had an eagerness for life, an openness to the world. Her boat was rented, and came with an oven the owner told her wasn't safe to use. The windows were lined with gaffer tape to stop them leaking. Jo worked with severely autistic adults, and I would go on to learn that she was always up for an adventure. Her heart would skip, working hard to keep up with her youth; grimy gigs, sleepless festivals, and food-less weekends in squatted flats.

We ate our eggy bread and sipped tea on the roof, staring out over the still water with rubbish gathering in corners, our backs to the constant stream of cyclists and hordes of Sunday strollers on the canal path.

"Thanks, Jo. Now I need to go and empty my toilet."

"So do I! Let's go together."

We loaded up our boxes of poo onto wheels, and trailered them along the towpath behind us with Mango running closely alongside, through the middle of Zone 1, to the smelly disposal point. When we got back, Jo fired up her engine ready to cruise to Victoria Park. I had planned to walk to Broadway Market and so I hitched a ride, holding her torch as she steered through the Islington tunnel. I immediately loved Jo. She was funny, positive, smiley, and completely herself. London didn't tire her out, it energised her. She was humble, and she was brilliant.

Years of living in this unnatural city had left me feeling mismatched and longing for connection. But now the waterways were making things clearer. The city's rivers and canals were helping me to start finding my pack.

Rain. I watched the drops plop into the Regent's Canal, bouncing on greeny black. It was mesmerising. Up above, grey mixed into grey, the sky one big blend of cloud, looming over the water. Rain began to blow horizontally as I crossed the bridge. The clouds whipped up a more furious wild wind, which lashed my ears and made everything sound different. Autumn was getting colder, and wetter. I walked faster along the towpath to get to my home, which was now in Mile End – *Genesis* was moored next to The Palm Tree, a diamond-in-the-rough pub that had survived the heavy World War 2 bombing of this area, where the same old boys played jazz every week and pints could only be paid for in cash. I was almost home. I walked past boaters as they covered their work benches and generators with tarp. Just like the river workers of days gone by, they were bargees cut off from land, and the shelter it provided in wet weather.

The muddy boots and wellies I kept just inside *Genesis'* front door made my home feel tiny and shed-like. After all, it was the size of some people's porch to their house. I battened down the hatches against the sploshing rain. Through the window I could see a pair of clumsy round coots, white billed and flapping, were enjoying the downpour. Despite being sheltered, I was unable to get away from it. On board *Genesis* I was having to get used to the fact that I could hear, feel and see the weather much more than I ever could in a flat or house. But I liked it. It awakened my connection with the outdoors.

That night I woke to the ringing plinking sound of metal echoing into the air. Silence. And then a low, metallic clinking again. My eyes slowly adjusted to the low light, my ears noticing the other sounds: wind, rain hitting the low metal roof two feet from my head, boat fenders squeaking along the concrete bank. *Ah, I know that sound.* The clanging was mooring pins being hammered into the ground with heavy mallets – a sound only too familiar for me from all the times I had moved *Genesis*. Reluctantly, I forced myself out of bed and found my wellies. Outside, the storm was bracing and the wind sharp. I readjusted a couple of fenders to stop the boat scraping and clonking along the concrete edge. Up the towpath I could see my neighbours bashing their steel mooring pins deeper in to the mud with mallets. They wanted to make sure their homes were secure. The storm that had whipped up was wanting to take our ships with it; it would succeed with some. *Please stay in, hold my home*, I thought as I hammered metal into sodden mud and retied boat ropes in the dark. Cursing loudly, I went back inside and finally got into bed, pissed off and damp. I went to sleep not knowing whether *Genesis* would still be in the same place in the morning.

Our floating homes were without foundations, and on nights like this it became even more apparent. There were no heavy barbed anchors to secure them. A bulldozer would not be required to destroy our bobbing abodes, just the momentary loosening of woven hemp or polypropylene, a sharp bread knife to a line, or a particularly strong wind. Easily frayed braided threads were all that attached us to this world, a couple of hitches of permanence, a few loops of security. I had been enjoying how easy it was to untie the ropes and float off somewhere new. But that night I felt too unbound and untethered, aware that my life was secured with a knot.

I stared down at the featureless desk. On it was a glass of water, a pot of pencils, a microphone, some buttons and a lamp. I was sitting inside the giant fish-tank of a soundproof box, alone and exposed. I thought about how to introduce the next TV show to try to persuade viewers to keep watching. Headphones on, microphone adjusted, levels checked, script scribbled on – words underlined, crossed out, circled – shoulders rolled back.

"And five, four, three…"

The TV show's credits rolled. The voice in my ears was my cue to take a breath, push the little mic fader up and read the short, friendly script I'd written. It was my last live continuity announcement of the night.

"And the drama continues next Wednesday night at eight. Don't move a muscle, as coming up next, the new series of…"

Mic fader down, headphones off, pick up bag, and silently leave the studio was how it went after these late shifts. Then out into the dark of an autumn evening.

"Hello," I'd say to the driver of the paid-for taxi waiting for me outside, the first words spoken to an actual person in hours. My voice was reaching millions, but I'd spent most of the day almost entirely alone, at high risk of catching the plague of social isolation, the sickness of the lonely digital age, supposedly deadlier than obesity or smoking fifteen fags a day. The driver would nod, a half-glance at me in his rear-view mirror, as I'd sink into the black leather back seat and watch the busy night whizz past. After an hour the car would slow, and the faceless driver, still looking straight ahead, would mumble, "Er, is this where you want dropping, is this… the right address?" Not waiting for an answer, and assuming this wasn't where I lived, he'd start tapping at the map on his phone and looking out of his window at the nowhere place.

"Yes, thanks, this is fine, I'll get out here, bye." "OK," he'd say, without turning around. Once on the towpath and out of sight, I'd run over bridges to darkness, heart in my mouth but knowing there was no other way home. Even if I was moored up next to neighbours who would look out for me during the night, there was still the solitary walk back to the boat to face up to. One time that autumn it took me fifteen minutes to build up the courage to walk across one of the bridges that crossed over to the unlit Hackney Marshes. God knows who lay hidden in its darkness. I was panicking. My phone was dead, and no one was around. It took me a few more failed attempts to cross before I spotted a security man locking up at a recycling unit, next to a council dog pound and the sound of invisible, crying hounds. I shouted to him, and he said he'd walk me to the end of the bridge. It reminded me of another night not long before, when, too afraid to walk the long way along the dark towpath, a cab driver lowered me down by my arms from the road above onto the towpath close to my boat. Once over the bridge, I thanked the security man, and ran as fast as I could down the towpath. In a daze, I half-forgot where I was moored. I knew from stories that boaters I'd met had told me that there was a real risk of something happening to me. After all, I was residing in some of the most crime-stricken boroughs of London, and travelled home alone each night along the unlit treacle black river, which hid all sorts of horrors. Once, the body of a man and two headless bears had been found floating in these waters. Twitching trees and agile bats would catch my eyes and night sounds pricked my ears as I moved fast. My senses would become heightened and alert, animal-like.

I could only breathe freely again once I had entered the boat, locked the door behind me and cuddled Mango, who would be eagerly waiting for me. The release of emotion was like taking off an overpacked backpack, instant de-weighting and a change in bodily feeling. It would take a few minutes before I regained the nerve to take Mango out. This happened before I regained the nerve to take Mango out. This happened a lot. I could too quickly go from confident, chatty, young, professional to heart-pounding, vulnerable and convinced I was about to be attacked at any moment. At times, as the nights drew in and the fun of the summer seemed far behind me, this rollercoaster of feelings forced me to seriously ask myself, *Am I cut out to be a boater?*

It was the kind of scream that you rarely hear, the kind where you know something really bad has happened. I was inside my boat alone when I heard it. Mango jumped around my feet, whirling around. I grabbed the whistle I kept to call for help in emergencies and bolted out of the front door to look around. At first I couldn't see anyone. I scanned the water around each boat, and then I could see a neighbour a few boats up, bent over, her face hidden in her hands. The screams were coming from her. My legs moved with speed I didn't know I had. I held her slim, shaking body tight.

"Tell me what's happened. Can you try and tell me what's happened?"

Her eyes were filled with tears and fear, her words confused and broken. By day she was a fiercely on-the-ball lawyer, and it was shocking to see her this fragile.

"I… I was walking Penny, in the marshes, just there, through the fence, no the… that gate thing, kissing gate. She ran into the trees after something, I kept calling her but she wouldn't come all the way back, and kept going into the trees."

She was looking down intently as she talked, as if visualising what had happened.

"It was like Penny was leading me to something. Then I saw a silhouette, a figure. There was a man, in the middle."

"In the middle of the path, a silhouette, a man with a rope in front of me. I was so scared. I told him I was sorry if Penny had scared him. I thought Penny had scared him. He was just standing there. The rope… the rope was tied to the tree. It was tied in a noose. He was about to hang himself."

My neighbour raised her gaze from the floor to me, her tears becoming heavier.

"I told him not to move, that I was going to get help, I didn't have my phone on me so I had to leave him. I untied the rope from the branch, it was really tight, it took me a few minutes, five minutes, I don't know, I kept telling him not to move, to stay there. Then I ran here. We have to go find him."

It took a frantic five minutes of running before we got to him, the man who had been just moments away from making the decision to pass from life to death. We sat with him under a tree, upon leaves and twigs catching our breath. Our arms held his body, and his hands rested tightly in ours. He sobbed, his hat dipped to cover his eyes.

"I miss my family. I'm sorry, I'm so sorry. My family are all in Turkey. I don't have anyone here. I'm sorry, I'm so sorry."

The green spaces that straddled the city's waterways had refreshed me. They had fed my insatiable desire for wild and rawness. They smelled of something other than public transport and clean recording studios. But that night they frightened me. This life on the edge, on the borough's boundaries, the city's liminal space, meant life was sometimes dangerously unpredictable. This place was not always life giving. It was a place where people with intentions you'd rather not think about could wander in the city's darkness, a place where people who didn't want to be found could hide. It was a place you could disappear, or lose yourself.

As the winter drew in and I felt more alone, I found it harder not to notice the muck *Genesis* was floating in. Not just in the canals but the river too. The River Lea, where I would often moor if I wanted to be close to Hackney, is one of the most polluted rivers in Britain, a poisoned, chemical-filled waterway. The water holds a concoction of road run-off, boat diesel, and tonnes of raw sewage from misconnected Victorian pipes that overflow into the Lea when it rains hard. The river sometimes fizzes and bubbles with gas created by rotting mush on its bed. It hides all sorts of secrets in its silent eerie black, and looking down into the diesel and sewage infusion it isn't hard to believe that, like hell's River Styx, if you drink from it you'll lose your voice for nine years. The Lea was once used to flush away East London's stink industries and as a dumping ground for human waste. In 1866 its soup of monstrous germs contaminated the area's drinking water with cholera and killed thousands of East Enders. Its waters fed the Thames, which once stank so much in the warmth of the summer sun that in 1858 the smell shut down Parliament.

As I lay in bed on *Genesis,* images of what might lie beneath me in the silty murk would float into my mind: shopping trolleys, broken bottles, pike, eels. And on those pitch-black nights my mind was also visited by fragments of buried memory that tried to rise through the sludge of my subconscious. It was frightening. I knew that if they managed to break through my well-built barricades and come into the light, I'd be flooded.

For thirteen years I'd kept a secret, scared that if I told it to anyone, it could open up wounds too messy to stitch back up. I had been fourteen when he swooped, hawk-like, I his prey clearly visible and easy to catch. I was sitting in the wide open. If I'd known then how exposed I was, perhaps I wouldn't have been so trusting. I wasn't a child, but I wasn't an adult. I was at that vulnerable and dangerous in-between time of being both a girl and a woman. Perhaps that's what allured him. Perhaps that's why I couldn't tell anyone about what was happening to me, my mind not developed enough to comprehend it.

Back then, when the handwriting in my school books slipped off the lines and the once-neat joined-up letters fell apart, after him, I avoided any solitary time. I filled up my head space and time with people. I didn't escape with chemicals and drink, too afraid that it would leave me vulnerable to mental illness, and I'd seen how debilitating depression was, how life sucking it can be. Instead I became addicted to company. As well as seeking distractions to prevent the tears from falling, there was so much to keep up with, get on with, to be and to do. There were first parties to go to, cigarettes to be shown how to inhale properly by a kid in the year above. Ben needed to be taken to The White Lion, where I could get served despite being well underage, while Dad cooled off after one of our arguments. My legs now needed to be shaved and the first shearing left me with a faint but permanent scar on my right shin. The electric fence at the car boot sale needed to be tested to see if it was *definitely* electric. The older man who appeared out of nowhere in the park and sat next to me on my blanket, rolling me a joint, needed brushing off. The light box by my mum's bed to keep her from slipping too low in winter needed to be made sense of. The smoke in my hair from the pub and the big bonfire of hedge-cuttings at the end of the garden needed washing out before school. There were songs from the school play to practise at lunch time on the school field. The back door from the kitchen onto the garden needed opening even though it was raining and cold out, as Mum needed air. She didn't like to feel trapped inside. GCSEs needed to be passed. Teachers had to be seen as the red ticks and "Good work" in my school books turned to "Please see me!", "Where is your homework?" Back then, there was no time for telling secrets.

Will I ever be able to say the words of what happened aloud, be able to tell someone, tell myself? I wondered, as I slipped into sleep, within my little home floating upon the dark waters of the River Lea.

Broad shouldered and sailor lean, Jake had chiselled cheeks, a strong nose and faded-blue eyes. His thick chin-length reddish-brown hair was tucked behind his ears, and he reminded me of a merman. When I first saw him, at the end of that first autumn, he was with two friends sitting on a colourful blanket on the grass in the gardens of an old church in Clapton, just a mile west of the River Lea, at a small, free one-day music festival. Something about this group stood out from everyone around. Mango, still young and small and running in every direction to say hello to everyone, went over to greet them, and we got chatting. They told me they were all back from various travels, were studying architecture and living in Hackney Wick. We talked. I don't know what about, but I remember smiling a lot. We all decided to go to The Dove on Broadway Market by the canal. We told stories as if we already knew each other. Jake had on well-worn jeans and a thick sage-green shirt, sleeves scrunched, under a thick knitted dark-blue jumper. Something about him felt warm and right. I told him I was moving my boat in a few days if he wanted to come and help. He said as long as there was toast and tea. He came and I showed him how to work a lock. After we moved *Genesis*, we drank tea inside.

This tall boy told me stories from his perch on the sofa. From under the bundle of blankets, he took my hand and held it tight. Time had all but stopped. When he left, his hug goodbye was longer than a friend's. I thought I would never see him again. That seemed to be how things went in this city. Then, the next day, there was a text. He asked if I wanted to go for a walk. I waited for him outside my boat with Matías, the Argentinian jewellery maker, who was moored nearby. Mango had been helping Matías pull in the punters all afternoon. Jake arrived at just after 5pm as he'd said he would, smiling. We walked and talked through Victoria Park. I wanted to hold his hand, it almost felt weird not to. As it got dark we ran around in the playground, hopping across wooden stumps and lying in a giant swinging basket with Mango between us. He kissed me. Gently. We got lost and swept away together.

I was in my mid-twenties and my heart was already overused, a single shake away from breaking. Like scavengers wanting flesh, London boys had ripped off pieces of me. I knew this time I must be more cautious. But this one, Jake, now lying in my bed after our first kiss, had appeared out of nowhere. Like the trees that lined the river, which relied on chance and a change in the wind and weather in order to pollinate, my own mating was also a random affair. But it felt right. He held me tight, toes touched toes, fingers locked under covers.

I would come to learn that Jake was a thinker – slow and steady, thoughtful, content. I'd soon discover he could walk or work for days on end without stopping. That he was obsessive about his studies and would often disappear into Architecture Land when he was up against deadlines to hand in portfolios. He was not flirty, had no ego and was in no way chaotic. I'd discover he was from the countryside, liked drizzly rain, maps, wooden things, hummus, salt and vinegar crisps, playing guitar, listening to bands and old songs that I'd never heard of, drawing and stories. I'd find out that he would bring stability, some smoothness to my waves. He gave me a book of fairytales. I thought it was the loveliest thing I'd ever been given.

This is where ours began, not like a Disney story but a real fairytale, one where everything is magical and strange, the love is true and pure, and the ending isn't necessarily happily ever after.

5

I was moored next to Victoria Park again, but it felt different now that it was really dark when I got home from work. Although this part of town was prime real estate, an address some people paid a lot of money for, by night, the park became an easy hangout for people with little else to do, and made for a convenient, unlit shortcut back to Hackney's estates. I was told this area was the most fiercely fought for among gangs in London, as it borders multiple boroughs. If you look online, there's a crime map of London's canals, with pins dropped where boaters have reported problems. I was now moored exactly where the majority of these pins were clustered, but I didn't know that then. I knew through word of mouth that at times it was sketchy here, but its beauty by daylight fooled me into thinking that perhaps it was now safer. One evening, I came home from work to find all my neighbours had moved on because of earlier break-ins that I'd heard about on the community Facebook group.

My boat was now totally alone. And so was I. Jake was in the middle of never-ending architecture deadlines. I knew he would be sleep-deprived in the studio in a focused state, powering through designs and sketches. Our time together so far had often been short, with many days passing between seeing each other. When he'd visit me we'd cook, talk, walk and laugh, and move my little boat to a new place. Our love was fresh, and our beginning was slow and precious; I couldn't call on him for help just yet. Exhausted, I weighed up whether I'd be safe here, just for the night. I could get up early, and move first thing, I told myself. But my gut said no. *Damn it.* I started the engine, untied the ropes, and wearily headed towards Mile End. Perhaps sensing my acute exhaustion, a night jogger, evidently not bothered by the pouring rain, opened one of the old lock gates at Old Ford for me, and I cruised through, peering from beneath my rain jacket hood. *Any spot will do tonight*, I told myself. I saw a gap in the row of boats, and raced to tie my boat up to the sodden bank in the black downpour. But in my rush, I slipped, jumping onto the wet metal of the gas locker, landing hard on the front deck on my bum. The pain took a while to ease enough for me to get up. "Go for a wee-wee Mango, quick, go for a wee-wee." My eyes scoured up and down the towpath repeatedly as I hurried him, my body exhausted, but knowing it needed to stay alert for just a little longer.

Wide awake and shaken from my long night, I lay in my bed, ears pricked to the sounds of night; someone's drunken phone conversation, a prowling fox, a rat ravaging the rubbish bag on the roof, which I still hadn't found a bin for. As well as the whistle that many boaters keep close to call for help if needed, my brother had made me order a red stain spray (a legal alternative to pepper spray), which would mark intruders if nothing else, as well as a foghorn and a crowbar which I kept in the little gap in the wood of the handmade bed behind my pillow. Knowing I had the crowbar quickly to hand made me feel less vulnerable. It didn't make me feel less afraid of being broken into, but it meant I knew what I would do if it happened: call Mango to me so he was safe, grab my crowbar and my whistle, go into the engine room and close the door, honk the boat horn and blow my whistle over and over.

Despite my difficult night, I was happy to be in Mile End. I felt a kind of affinity with it because I knew that my nan – my mum's mum – had grown up in East London. It felt good to be close to family history. Also, there were some good boat neighbours moored nearby. On one memorable wintry evening, I spotted Laurie ahead on the towpath. He was splitting wood with an axe and wedge, like a bronze-age woodsman thousands of years before. Power tools and metal engine parts were strewn across the towpath.

"I'm going to be a dad!" he told me when I stopped to say hello.

"That's amazing, Laurie!" I said.

Over the last couple of months, Laurie had become my walking boat bible, river guru, reassurance and technical advisor. We would bump into each other like this from time to time, and talk. The linear nature of a canal towpath makes regular serendipitous chats and crossing paths inevitable. Laurie was always as dirtied and oil-splattered as the tools he used to fix boats, his hands and long arms tanned and covered in paint. His brown hair had begun to form dreadlocks, and his handsome face had flecks of blue paint on it, like a docker who had been unloading indigo. To some he might have looked scruffy, but to me he looked admirable and honest. He passed on his vast boating knowledge freely, never summarising or patronising, explaining fully and in detail.

"Did you get my message about that DIY?" I took the opportunity to ask.

"Yes, sorry, I was meaning to reply. Right, you want to use this to sand those surfaces you were talking about," he said, brandishing a hefty-looking sander. "It'll be much better than what you've been using. Remember to oil it after, like I told you about before, rub it in, give it a few layers. For the chimney, you need to get hold of some fireproof rope, just tap it in with a screwdriver. Your windows will just need some new sealant which I think you said you've got, right?"

I'd quickly learned that being the owner of a boat meant a lot of maintenance and a constant to-do list of jobs. In a short amount of time, through necessity, the boat had forced me to become practical; it tested my strength, sanity and resilience. Daily routine changed with each place I moored up in, and there was always a lot to do. Wake up, find a secret gem of green space and go for an early morning walk with Mango, sometimes still in pyjamas, wash if there was enough water in the tank and I hadn't washed the day before, make breakfast and eat out on the deck if it wasn't raining, do a boat job or two like empty the toilet, go to a launderette, or cruise to fill up the water tank, chat with boaters on the towpath whilst looking for a bin to put a bag of rubbish into, find a café near the canal to write TV continuity scripts, cycle to the nearest tube station and travel to studios in Soho to do voice-overs, write in another café, travel to a TV channel for a continuity-announcer shift, do a small food shop, travel back to the boat and dangle shopping bags on bike handlebars, bump into boaters and share advice and stories, get home and haul bike onto boat roof, immediately take Mango for his second walk come rain or shine and enjoy some calm amongst nature, do some more boat jobs like check the batteries, grease the stern gland or change the gas bottles over, work out the logistics of the coming weekend's boat move, fix something that has decided to break, cook a big veggie supper and eat and drink with new boat neighbours either outside on a deck or on the towpath or squished into someone's boat, hang out with Jake when he arrives, talk, laugh, swirl around together on *Genesis*, sleep.

"Thanks Laurie. Appreciate it. I'll drop this back to your workshop when I'm done."

"No worries."

"And such lovely news that you're going to be having a boat baby! Esme. Beautiful name. Oh god, and sorry to hear of your near break-in. Did the police catch them?"

"No. And I followed the guys for forty-five minutes after I caught them on my boat. I was on the phone to the police the whole time describing what they looked like, where they were, telling them exactly what happened. Police didn't come. Didn't care. Said something about not knowing which borough I was in, so I gave up and went home to cook some sausages."

I shook my head. I was already only too aware of how difficult it was to call the police when you lived on a boat. Being off-grid and postcode-less often meant living on the border of London boroughs. In Hackney, with the Regent's Canal and River Lea forming the boundary between wards and councils, we were doubly on the edge, and no one's responsibility. It was only after a spate of violent muggings or rapes on or near the towpath that the law showed its face. Although on the waterways you could escape the ever-present feeling of being observed by the state, with that freedom came slow or non-existent police response to crime. Being nomadic didn't mix with other officialdom either, like bank accounts, voting, insurance, GP surgeries and HMRC. Answering "on a boat" when asked for my address, I had quickly discovered, made computers say No. Even though I was working, paying tax and national insurance and not breaking any law, being itinerant and without a land address made authorities suspicious. I used the postal address of a friend so I could be officially registered and receive the odd post whenever I was moored nearby. Other boaters used their parents' address, or used GP surgeries for the homeless, or ticked "no fixed address" with details of a place they have a connection with, such as a boatyard, so they were still able to vote.

Laurie and I said our goodbyes, and I headed home.

When I got back, I sat doubled over in stinging pain, on my Porta Potti, trying to wee. For the past couple of days I had been aware of a slight burning when I went to the loo but this was of a different magnitude. *Maybe if I sit in the bath, it won't hurt so much.* The water tank was low, but I didn't have it in me to cruise to the nearest tap, so I ran myself a shallow puddle to sit in.

I wanted to call Jake. I deliberated for a while about whether I should disturb him from his studies, and then gave in. I told him I was feeling unwell. He cycled to the boat and dropped off some soup, bread, lemon and ginger tea. He took Mango out for a quick walk to wee, heated up the soup which I didn't eat. I lay with my head on his lap whilst he talked about all sorts of interesting and clever things that I didn't understand whilst I drifted in and out of sleep. I knew he had to go. He had more deadlines. I told him I'd be OK.

I got worse. I started to cry with pain. I needed to see a doctor. I called the NHS advice line, feverish, shivering, confused and crying. Things were worse than I thought: a combination of a lack of drinking water, frequently holding in the urge to wee to save the space in my toilet for emergency night visits and a new lover had given me cystitis, which had turned into a kidney infection. Given that I was born with just one kidney, this wasn't great. My body shook with clammy fever, and I began feeling delirious. Soon the paramedics were by my boat. They'd arrived in someone's speedboat because they couldn't find me by road.

"I have a puppy, I can't go into hospital," I explained in desperation, doubled over in searing pain. "Please, can't I just have some antibiotics?"

"I'll look after your puppy," said my moustachioed neighbour Tim, overhearing my protests and leaning out of his widebeam. His bushy grey facial hair made him look like an eccentric army general from years gone by. "Don't you worry about a thing. I'll work it all out," he reassured me as I hobbled towards an ambulance in the Palm Tree car park.

Tubes pumped drugs into my veins in hospital, and after a few days Holly picked me up. She arrived with grapes and chocolates and took me home to *Genesis*, where my well-looked-after Mango was waiting for me. I still felt unwell but was far better than a few days before. I probably should still have been in hospital but had managed to persuade the doctor to release me early with a load of antibiotics because there was too much to do, and only me to do it. All I wanted to do was to curl up and sleep. But I had to go to work the next day and so needed to do a clothes wash. I was already wearing the same pants and socks twice, and god knows when the last time was that my jeans had been washed. A large rucksack filled with dirty clothes sat beside my bed waiting to be lugged to a launderette. I needed to empty my full loo. The nearest Elsan disposal point at Victoria Park was blocked again so I'd have to wee in the sink for tonight. Mango needed his two long walks a day, and feeding, I couldn't just let him out onto the towpath without me. I needed to run the engine as the batteries were getting low – if I didn't they would stop holding their charge as well and I would have to buy new ones. I needed to decide where I was going to go next, my two weeks here were almost up. I knew I really, really needed to learn how to make a fire. The temperature had dropped. The very last of autumn was falling. It had blown away without me noticing, and winter was about to take over. I was nowhere near ready.

I could see my breath as I lay in my bed. A couple of months had passed and the air had chilled, crisped, sharpened. My attempt at a fire must have gone out in the night. *Damn it.* Through the brass porthole I noticed a thin layer of ice around the hulls of the other narrowboats, topping the water like a crème brûlée crust. The winter sunlight, low and blinding, shone through the window. Outside, the green towpath verges sparkled with microscopic flakes of ice. *I'll get proper curtains before winter,* I'd promised myself. But winter had snuck in too quickly. I piled clothes on top of my pyjamas, took a deep breath and excavated myself from underneath two plump, feather-filled duvets. With my jumper, thick socks, scarf and hat, I was ready for my arctic expedition to the kitchen. Mittens on, I filled up the kettle and waited for the steam to thaw out my icy home.

I was discovering there were a lot of things I needed to learn for winter, like how to avoid getting numb, red fingers from pulling wet ropes, or how to arrive at work without coal dust under my nails, as well as how to find a way to stop Mango hiding my gloves. I needed to learn to always load more coal into the stove before bed. I needed to learn and master the art of layering pieces of wood and coal in perfect quantities to tempt the flames into behaving. *Today, today I might do better,* I thought. The fire-lighter packet was empty. I should have bought more. I scrunched up newspaper balls and placed bits of kindling on top, but the paper burned out before the wood took light. I wondered if the wind whistling down the chimney was too strong, or if the rain had got into the coal bag that I kept on the roof. I went outside to get a different bag in case it was drier. Tiptoes on the gunwale, I heaved it along the roof then tried to lift it down. Big black nuggets hit my body and rolled down me before splashing into the canal. The plastic bag had split and half of it was now in the water. "FUUUCK." I was defeated. I had been making pretty unsuccessful fires for weeks and this was yet another failed attempt. I went back inside, lit the oven, opened the door wide, and sat on the kitchen floor, with my body as close to the warmth of the flames as possible, risking carbon monoxide poisoning for instant warmth. My body ached from curling up to keep warm in bed, and, even though I had not managed to light a decent fire, somehow coal dust coated every surface. Mango's sooty paw prints were all over the small floor. I put my coat on and started writing TV continuity announcements for my live shift later. I typed until my fingers were so cold they hurt.

That night, just as I had thought the day was over, Mango, who was sitting in his favourite place on the top step, tilted his head to the side at me – a sign I knew only too well. *You want to go out again?* I thought. As I opened the doors to step outside my muscles braced for even more of a chill, but it was the same temperature out as it was in. Standing on the bow of my boat, I felt like I'd gone back in time to Victorian London, with its noxious fumes and dimly lit walkways. Along the canal, hazy smoke chugged from more successful chimneys than mine, and the towpath smelled of hot dinners and a faint smog. A lot of the boats had no lights on, which made me wonder if many jumped ship in the winter months for somewhere warmer, leaving their vessels to sit alone, cold. Given courage by the lack of people, a stealthy city fox trotted past me in search of some bin-scavenged dinner. I stayed on the boat to admire her, nocturnal and savvy. Her super-sensitive hearing meant that she, along with around ten thousand other foxes, was able to roam the streets of the capital, hardly noticed. Like the country's railway tracks and motorway verges, the towpaths contained a wealth of resilient wildlife. The fox quickstepped to the yard behind a German bakery before disappearing.

Perhaps Mango hadn't realised we'd moved the previous night, or that the towpath edge was now a foot or two higher than before, because he judged his leap to land badly. With a dramatic splash, Mango was now neither on the bank nor in the boat, but almost completely submerged in the near-freezing cold canal. *Shit.* He started swimming in circles, looking up at me frantically, but I couldn't reach his collar from the stern – the water level was too low. Starting to feel the flush of panic, I hopped back over to the bank. Lowering myself down, and covering my last clean jumper in a layer of dirt, I grabbed a clump of weeds as a hold, and leaned towards my dog, but my fingertips could only brush the top of his fur. Mango kept swimming round and round, surely tiring himself out. *How long can he keep himself up?* There was only one thing to do, and it would not be pleasant. Wellies off, socks off, hat off, scarf off, jumper off, thermal top off, jeans off.

"Mango, come," I said in a bright and breezy tone, to try and make him calm, as if this was all no big deal. I lowered myself into the polluted canal. The winter water was just above waist height, and my feet tip-toed over the squidgy ground underneath. The cold stung my entire body. "Good boy, good boy," I panted softly, trying not to think of eels and leeches and boggy riverbed bugs. Finally, I firmly grabbed the bundle of soggy curls and, raising him high above my head, shoved him back onto the slippery stern. He shook himself dry in line with my face. I was out of there before I even knew how.

I stepped back inside *Genesis*, which rocked and creaked as a boat went past, driving through the dark. I wondered whether the boater steering had seen my nighttime dip. I dried off and put all my layers back on, including my coat and hat, and tried again to light a fire. Scrunched up newspaper, wood kindling and lumps of coal. *I have to do this.* I thought back to what a boat neighbour, a man in his fifties who ran a café from his boat, had told me a few days before. "You need to really load it up with coal. Don't be sparing. When you're making a fire, throw on loads of coal, you want one big pile glowing red. Just keep feeding it, keep it burning, don't let it go out." I did what he had said, and soon, a throbbing orange glow shone through the glass of the stove. I managed the draught through air dials, added more coal and a log to the pile until it roared red, and the air around it was thick with heat. A primal satisfaction hugged me. I had done it. I was filled with a sense of meaningfulness and achievement from heating my home that was incomparable to the feeling of turning up the thermostat a notch.

As the boat slowly thawed and my hunched shoulders began to drop, I filled the kettle and waited for its urgent hissing scream before filling two hot-water bottles and tucking them beneath the duvet of my bed. I wanted to wash but couldn't bear to expose my skin to any cold again. The air around the stove was warming up, but in the bedroom the sheets were still so freezing they felt wet. My breath steamed into the biting air. I was cocooned within a multitude of layers: thermals, hot water bottles, two duvets, the air within the boat, the insulation beneath the interior wood cladding, the steel shell of the boat. But I was still cold. The water's chill had penetrated my insides. The outdoors had become part of me. In the night I woke coughing and wheezing, a deep full-bodied chesty spluttering that exhausted my stomach muscles. Each rasp jolted my neck. Perhaps the damp coldness had seeped too deep into my lungs. Perhaps I had breathed in too much soot and ash from the wood burner. I fell back asleep.

I woke in the morning to a canal thinly topped with a fresh frozen crust, the ice holding litter and leaves. The stinging nettles at the canal's edge looked diamond-encrusted, the grass crunchy white, and the water looked as if it was wearing a blanket of misty milk, hazily reflecting bare-branched skeleton trees. But despite the bite outside, for the first time in my first winter, I woke to a warm boat, a few lumps of coal in the stove still glowing.

The tiller was cold to hold and the air was sharp against my face, but thermal layers kept my body warm. The city's towers stood silhouetted against a sky of long, thin clouds lit up in gold. A cup of tea sat atop the condensation-covered roof as I cruised along the waterway that is London's back door to Essex and Hertford, the Lee Navigation. The Lee Navigation was built parallel to the Old River Lea to shorten the route and allow barges to carry goods from Hertford down to London and vice versa. The Lee and the Lea meet and become one below the Lea Bridge Road, and there's little consistency in the spelling. There is evidence of this waterway's use for transportation from as far back as the Bronze Age.

I moored up next to the twelve-billion-pound Olympic Park built upon a hundred tonnes of radioactive waste in an area where London's filthiest slums once stood. Behind it was the late Zaha Hadid's Aquatics Centre and the ArcelorMittal Orbit. They hid a complex network of waterways called the Bow Back Rivers, then closed off to boaters to allow for Olympic legacy work and the construction of Crossrail. This tangle of waterways at Hackney Wick once provided water to mills and industry. With the rise of electrical power and cars in the twentieth century, the Wick and its waterways fell into disrepair, becoming an industrial graveyard. From the early 70s, it became a place for travelling families to call home, on two official council-run sites. But with the 2012 Olympic construction, the land was grabbed, and I'd read that the English Romany Gypsies of Clay Lane and the Irish Travellers of Waterden Crescent who'd lived in their homes legally for generations were forced to live amongst a dusty demolition site before being moved off to new sites, which weren't ready and were in places they did not know. Families and communities were broken up. Continuous cruisers were also moved out of central London during the Olympics. It wasn't just homes here that were lost for two weeks of sport: forty-five hectares of wildlife-rich marshes, nature reserves and fields were also destroyed.

I turned off the engine and a noisy nearby motorway hummed in my ears. Home was now a graffitied maze of rubbish tips, car garages and factories, and in a place once left behind but rapidly being rediscovered. Hackney Wick was where the party was at. In disused warehouses and old factories where plastic, confectionery, toys and dyes were once produced, artists now lived, DJs played, and bars and cafés were popping up.

As I put the kettle on, Mango's ears pricked at the sound of the coal boat. He looked at me to let me know he'd heard something. I thanked him. I never knew when a coal boat was coming, they didn't seem to have a schedule, but I'd learned to recognise the sound of their engines pop-popping and would race outside to grab their attention and stock up with supplies. The coal boat had an almost samba band sound, an irregular rhythm. The noses of a pair of heavily laden work boats came into view through the window. I flicked the hob off and bolted back outside. "Can I get some coal?" I shouted to the coal man. He nodded and, with just a single hand, steered his home and business – probably almost fifty tonnes of vessel and cargo put together – closer to *Genesis*. His two boats were coupled up with lines, and he moved them effortlessly. One had a motor; the other was a 'butty', the name for a narrowboat without an engine. These coal-laden boats sit much deeper in the water and, with just one off-centre propeller between them, they must be quite the art to master. He began loading sooty bags onto my roof with blackened hands. Like trained sheep dogs, his boats seemed to understand exactly what their master required of them, and stayed perfectly steady despite only being loosely tethered to *Genesis*. I noticed the cracks on the coal man's skin, deeply engrained with soot.

"Can I get gas and a top-up of diesel too?" I asked. He got to work with a kind smile.

"It's a good idea to fill the diesel tank up to the top in winter. Helps prevent condensation. Water in the tank can lead to diesel bug."

"OK, fill her up, thanks."

When it came to loading the gas canister onto *Genesis'* front deck, his boats slowly inched further forwards without him at the stern so he could reach more easily. In a soft, blunt pencil he wrote "*Genesis*" in the column titled "Address" of his book, which already looked like it belonged in a museum, and the amount in another column. We talked for a short while about old boats and dogs, the last coal man, the cherrywood he was burning and the divers looking for something at the dodgy lock. I thanked him and paid him and he chugged away. I listened to the *pop pop pop popping* fading as he drifted downstream. The man my warmth relied on.

"Let's build a little, little home with a big, big outdoors," Jake said, as he stopped playing a tinkering tune on the guitar. I was now moored north of Hackney Wick, where he lived on land, on the River Lea beside Hackney Marshes. There were fewer cycling commuters and the flocks of tourists seemed to not venture there. I liked it, with its overgrown riverbank and water levels that fluctuated with rainfall. I liked the gentle flow of the river rather than the stillness of the canal. Jake was lying on his back on the sofa, his legs over my lap, the guitar on his broad chest. I'd lost track of how long we'd been chatting. It amazed me how our bodies fitted so comfortably on that small sofa, neither of us in the least bit bothered at the confined space of the boat. God, I loved him.

"Beside a river, or near the sea?" I said. "Then I can swim every day?"

"Yep, and we can have a garden for bonfires. And there will be hills, and a forest."

I spotted Mango stealthily stealing one of the little pieces of kindling from the basket beside the lit stove and taking it to his bed to add to his collection.

"He thinks I haven't noticed," I said.

Outside was crisp, but inside the air was thick with heat from my well-stocked fire, and the low winter sun streamed through the window onto Jake's face and up onto the curved wooden-clad roof above us. A patterned piece of material used as a makeshift curtain was rolled up above the frame. Jake sat up and put the guitar down. We faced each other cross-legged, in a swirl of colourful woollen blankets.

"Can we have a cabin in the garden for friends to come and stay, and space for them to pitch up tents? And a bath outside? And lots of lanterns and trees?" I asked, smiling. Perhaps he thought this was make-believe, but for me it was real. I still wanted that home one day, even though this was more a home to me than anything had been before.

"Yes. And we can have a canoe or a little boat for adventures. And we won't have to wear shoes very often. And we can spend days drinking coffee and reading and walking."

"And a kitchen with a big wooden table, and all our neighbours can pop over for tea. And flowers everywhere."

We talked like this sometimes, but without talking practicalities or entering into any grown-up conversation about the future, how we'd make any dreams come true. We were different in that way: he could just imagine, I wanted to make things happen.

Mango started playing with his toy, throwing it up and then catching it, putting it under cupboards to then try and get it out again. He was always full of beans.

"He's still not tired," I said. "I don't think I'll ever be able to wear him out. I've already taken him out for about an hour this morning. Oh, I forgot to tell you, last night it was pouring so hard that when I woke up there were drips coming through the air vent onto my face."

"Maybe you could sleep with a brolly over you?"

I smiled. "Fancy another walk? Mango needs to burn off some more energy."

"Yep." He picked up our little blue cups with dribbles of cold tea in them off the floor and put them by the sink.

"I'll make us supper when we get back," Jake said. "Roast up some veg or something, or make some kind of spicy beany stew thing. Oh, I drew you this." He pulled out a small piece of watercolour paper from his back jeans pocket, with a pen sketch of a little mouse with big eyes. I thanked him and tucked it into the corner of a picture frame on the wall, along with other small bits of paper with things he'd drawn and words he'd written for me. I loved all of the little notes and sketches he gave to me. He didn't have a smartphone, avoided texting as much as possible, and barely ever used Facebook. Our love felt more of a different time. We weren't constantly in touch on our phones, we were either spending time together in person, or missing each other if we were apart for a while. So instead of phone messages, I had these little notes. One of them he gave to me when I went on a very long walk.

adventure strong and adventure slow
your mind and feet know where to go

tramp through fog and tramp through snow
your boots will feel the earth below

rough like stone and tough like rock
people forget their doors unlock

over the hearth and through the marsh
there's love outside where nature laughs

Jake threw on his coat and wrapped the scarf that I had knitted him around his neck twice. It was red and orange like fire, woolly and chunky, with soft rows of loose loops then neater ones, the edges wobbling in and out. It was the first and only thing I have ever knitted. I grabbed my keys which were attached to a floating cork ball – designed to make sure dropped keys floated – from the hook by the door, and accidentally kicked over the dog bowl of water again.

Outside, the air bit. But the blue sky was quickly turning grey and, without much warning, turning into one big storm cloud. Mango ran in every direction, sniffing everything. We ducked behind a brick wall into the Middlesex Filter Beds, walking around a raised circle of concrete, moss-covered remains of cast-iron machinery and an industrial Stonehenge-type formation of stone blocks which were the foundations of an old engine house. The information board explained that the Filter Beds were originally built in the mid-1800s to filter water through layers of gravel and sand after London's worst outbreak of cholera took over 14,000 lives. They were closed in the 1960s and nature took over; they were now filled with wildlife, making a green lung in the city. It was quiet, a world away from the bustle of nearby Clapton. The greenness of this secret place, set within the wet isolated marshlands of East London, felt very wild.

We weaved our way through the old stone structures out onto the grasses of Hackney Marshes. Mango raced across the damp grass. He showed me a fairy ring of mushrooms. Goalposts and electricity pylons decorated the enormous open space, home to over eighty grass football and rugby pitches. For centuries this was where locals grazed their animals. It was a place where landowners would allow commoners to cultivate during harsher, less profitable months. Mango raced ahead, then stopped at a line of trees and turned back to check if he could go further. I told him to wait. I didn't know what was beyond there. As Jake and I reached Mango, we saw a smaller winding waterway. "Ok, Mango, go on," I said, thinking at least the water would clean off some of the mud which he seemed to be constantly half-covered in. Not having a garden tap to hose him off during winter or enough water to regularly bath him, I'd accepted he'd just have to be a scruffy dog, and like me, not as clean as the other city dwellers.

This waterway looked wilder, not man-made. It was the old River Lea, which forks off the navigable cut that *Genesis* was moored on. It looked magical, a world away from the housing estates of Homerton on the other side of the wet border. Over its shallows, bare willow trees drooped. I spotted a shoal of small fish swimming in swirls. Mango found a stick he liked and dropped it by Jake's feet, asking him to throw it into the water for him. As they played fetch, I wandered through the patch of woodland which ran alongside the river. There was an ancient-looking tree, split as if lightning had struck it, one of its leafless branches dangling loose and only just managing to hold onto the trunk. Rarely in London do you find yourself entirely alone. But in this moment, it was just me, and a silent tree. I stopped, and found myself soothing it, telling it not to worry, that things were OK. I noticed then that I had changed. I now felt a part of my surroundings, more connected to the nature that surrounded me. I was paying more attention, like I did when I was a kid. I felt the tree's ridges and bumps, and ran my fingers over its textured, burnt-looking split bark. The grey cloud above exploded.

I walked back to where Jake and Mango were still playing fetch, Mango swimming and shaking off cold water from sodden curls, in utter heaven. We were quickly becoming soaked, and decided to turn around. We walked back to the boat through the downpour, looking as unwashed and unbrushed, as bedraggled and tangled as each other, but none of us caring one bit. Somehow, in this watery world, even the cold winter rain could be beautiful. We reminisced about our adventure to the very top of Scotland a few months before, where we'd joined Jake's dad on a tiny sailing boat. We talked about a long-distance walk we were planning, along the coast of Turkey, and decided we'd pack light, and wild camp the whole way. As we reached the river, I saw a rogue boat floating free. Its pins must have come loose from the sodden mud. I rescued it by jumping aboard, throwing one of the ropes to Jake on the bank then pulling it in. After so many boat moves already, this felt incredibly natural and intuitive. It felt good to know what I was doing. By the time we got back to *Genesis* the cloud had run dry, and London was left lit up and orange. Its sounds dampened to a softer melody as the sun began to set, creating a glowing stripe up the river.

6

"Where do you think they fell? About here?" asked Dan, a boater I hardly knew but who had immediately come to my rescue. My keys had fallen from my jeans pocket as I'd hopped across his boat to *Genesis*. The single cork ball hadn't stopped them from sinking; I'd need to remember to buy a double-cork keyring. Now my keys were sitting somewhere on the sludge at the bottom of the canal. Dan was fresh-faced and clean. His tidiness and enthusiasm made him look and sound like a new boater even though I don't think he was. He plopped his powerful sea magnet, usually used for recovering things from the bottom of the sea, into the canal and swept the rope around the bow, back and forth, pulling it out and then throwing it in again. He fished confidently, like a snake charmer, as if he knew – even though it was unlikely – that the water would provide my shiny keys. My eyes wandered to a Kraken made from multi-coloured rope on the bow of his boat. The giant squid-like sea-monsters lived in the deep of the ocean off the coasts of Iceland and Norway, and were the stuff of seafaring legend, feared for attacking pirate ships.

"I crocheted it myself," Dan said, noticing that I was admiring it. It must've taken him weeks.

Raw with cold, I rubbed my red fingers together and pulled my sleeves over them. The winter air scratched my lungs as I breathed. He fished the magnet out again, no luck. Then in and back out a few times.

"Ahaa." He pulled the rope up and a shiny set of keys was stuck to the bottom of the horseshoe-shaped metal. "There you go," he beamed, as he passed them to me.

Dan didn't owe me anything, had no favour to return. He was just helping out a fellow boater, another member of the same tribe. Until then, we'd only had short chats as we came and went. For a week my boat had hugged his with its ropes, *Genesis* double-moored on the outside, hidden from the towpath behind his boat. When I hadn't been able to find a place to moor, I'd pulled up alongside his boat, knocked on the door, and asked if it would be OK to double-moor, if he'd mind my boat obstructing his views on to the water, checking when he was planning on moving. He was friendly and said he didn't mind at all. Generally this was the way it went, and generally boaters kept to an etiquette of not double-mooring at antisocial hours. If I needed to double-moor and someone wasn't in, I'd leave a note asking if it was OK. If a boater needed to double-moor me I'd help line their boat up and tie ropes. Moving the boat when moored on the inside of another boat required some clever rope skills, carrying a dog and bike across another boat when moored on the outside took some balancing. But more often than not friendships were formed through having such close neighbours for a short time. My brief conversations with Dan had been comforting, offering familiarity in a constantly shifting life. I would not have a chance to repay him, but I'd go on to help another boater out, who'd then help another. That was the way it went.

Not long after Dan found my keys, it was time for him to move on. I gave him a hand, holding long ropes and hammering pins back into mud before going inside. But then, to my own confusion, I suddenly found myself sobbing on *Genesis'* cold, soot-covered floor. I loved the variety, the impromptu spontaneity of each day, but for once I just wanted something, one thing, to stay the same for a little longer. This stranger and his boat were gone, and I momentarily felt left out at sea, a castaway, in Hackney's waters.

Jake wasn't around, he had his head deep in Architecture Land. We'd see each other soon for a few days. He was going to show me his favourite camping spot in the Lake District, where he'd spent his childhood summer holidays. But right now, with deadlines for his architecture studies continually looming, he'd disappeared for a bit. I knew he would be sleeplessly drawing and drinking coffee in his bedroom, the Architecture Jungle, in his rented Hackney Wick house which he shared with two other architecture students, the owner of a travelling pop-up opera company, a drag-queen and a singer. The walls of his room were covered in wonderful sketches and intricate drawings printed on huge sheets, while in the corners were a few musical instruments, a perfect source of procrastination. Jake's desk was made from a door he'd found in the street and was crowded with model buildings, a homemade 3D printer and a mockup of an expanding festival dome. On shelves were books with words I didn't understand, notebooks stuffed with a million ideas, and in the corner a huge, whirring computer. I thought about calling him and asking if I could come over to his, have a night of respite from my semi-camping life and luxuriate in the shower, do a clothes wash in his washing machine. I had done this a few times before, but I didn't want to break his concentration.

Maybe I'll give up and rent a room, I thought to myself. *No, that would be shit.*

I remembered what it was like to live in shared houses. I thought of the alternative housing solutions of some of my friends. One of them lived in a garden shed, another dwelled in an actual windowless cupboard for months. One friend lived in her van. Other friends were Property Guardians of unused buildings, often old Victorian social housing due for demolition, to keep squatters out. It was a 'cheaper' alternative to London living, but came with just one month's security at a time. It often meant living in mouldy, dust-mite-infested tower blocks with broken windows and no hot water or heating; empty Victorian terraces with exposed tangled electricity wires, ovens that were unsafe to use and loos that didn't flush properly; forgotten nurseries with high ceilings and rainbows painted on the walls; tired care homes with strange hospital-style disabled bathrooms. Other friends lived in warehouses, with windowless units that housed anything from five to twenty people, a mixture of ordinary grafters on low salaries, artists, hippies, and posh people pretending to need to rough it. Through the makeshift cracker-thin plywood walls you could hear the sounds of the party next door, the love-making upstairs, the loud machinery and factory buzzing outside, and the strangers in the communal area taking drugs. Socialising and conversations at any time unavoidable, privacy hard to grab. No, my boat was what I needed.

I told myself there were just a few more weeks left of lighting the fire in the morning. That things would be easier when the cold months were over. Keeping warm would be one less thing to worry about. After a long winter, a coal-dust-free zone was finally in sight. I would enjoy safer bike rides home in daylight, banishing my ugly jumpers and thermal layers back under my bed. Boat moves, trips to launderettes, emptying the toilet wouldn't be in the cold and wet. The doors and windows of my tiny home could be opened. Crocuses and daffodils would grow.

Sometimes, when I couldn't sleep on *Genesis* that winter, I would count the different homes I'd had and try to remember whether I'd ever felt at home in any of them. After Dad left when I was eleven, and Ben and I went to stay with him every other weekend, his home was constantly changing. There was the room in an elderly couple's house first, where Dad and I made cookies. There was the one-bedroom basement flat he rented. The kitchen was so tiny that only one of us could go in at a time and the sofa-bed that I slept on took up the whole lounge. There was the girlfriend's house which was half-an-hour's drive away. She had a sister who was a millionaire and had a swimming pool in her garden and gold taps. If we told Mum about it she got sad. There was the other rented house in the next town where he smashed a mug on the kitchen floor because Ben and I had not done the washing up, or something. He then moved into the house of a girlfriend who had children. In between this, we were at Mum's.

By the time I was a young teen, I stopped going to Dad's every other weekend. I'd kill time talking to strangers after school, end up going to the houses of people I'd just met on the train to smoke weed. I didn't want to go home. Home wasn't home anymore, Mum's or Dad's. I'd lost Dad to his affair and girlfriends and lost Mum to low times I couldn't understand. Mum would either be so sad or overwhelmed she couldn't talk, or be working twelve-hour shifts. Lies to Mum about where I was at night were causing regular arguments. I became reckless. I said yes to everything. I said yes to things I wouldn't have, if I'd only known better.

I wondered how things got so bad with my dad. When I was little I used to sit with him by rivers and lakes for hours whilst he fished. We would watch hedgehogs eat the cat food we had left out for them in the garden at night. He had told me stories of a princess who lived in a castle on a cloud, and given me a special stone with crystals inside it that a fairy in the woods had given him. He made me a treasure hunt and hid one of the clues under a flowerpot with a real frog. Now I hardly saw him. Other young urbanites I knew were kept afloat by short escapes to their parents. "Going back *home* this weekend," they'd say, returning well slept, fed and charged. Not being from anywhere, and without an escape cord to pull for a place to stop and take a break from all the adapting, I could feel myself beginning to wear down.

I banished all thought of these different homes on land, homes that were not my own. I now had solace, a floating home of my own. And after all, I was getting the hang of off-grid nomadic boat life. The layers of my knowledge were building, and I was finding it easier to solve all the logistical puzzles: What's my journey to work this week? Where can I next get water from? How much gas is left in the canister? Do I need to get some more coal soon? How are the batteries doing? Is the toilet almost full? Where am I next going to moor? Will there be space? When can I move? When have I got time to go to the launderette? Where is the launderette?

Further back in my mind, but still there nonetheless and taking up space, were the less frequent considerations: Where shall I get the hull blacked with bitumen? When can I take a few days off to get the boat to the boatyard for craning to get work done? Where will I buy replacement batteries when they stop holding their charge as well? Who should I book to do the next boat safety certificate? Which weekends can I put aside for boat jobs? When will I get to top up with diesel? Which electricians or engineers could help fix that thing? There was also the never-ending to-do list squished up in there too: sand and treat rust, clean bilge, seal windows, sweep chimney, check the inspection hatch in the floorboards to see if the internal hull is dry, clear the propeller of plastic bags and river weed through the weed hatch at the stern, check the engine oil and water. And of course the usual household to-do list to keep in mind: food shop, tidy, clean, cook, walk Mango, feed Mango, give Mango his monthly flea treatment. The markings on my mental map of the waterways needed space in my memory too: shallow bends, dodgy locks, bins, break-in hot spots, nearby cafés with Wifi, pubs with loos you could use without being noticed, canal banks with hidden concrete ledges beneath the water, noisy stretches near a road, benches where drinkers sit, low bridges and secret taps.

Although the list was endless, I was proud of the knowledge and skills I was developing. I liked how I was becoming fluent with it all and good at being a continuous cruiser, a liveaboard boater. I liked that it gave me a sense of purpose.

"Want any solar?" came a voice one day as I was sitting on the front deck of my boat. Spring had finally arrived and I was relieved to feel its warmth. It seemed the right moment to think about using the sun to power my boat's electrics. The voice belonged to a bloke called Dale who was cruising past on his boat and told me and my neighbours that he'd got hold of a load of huge solar panels, and was flogging them cheap. "Yes! Yes, I'll take one. How much?" I shouted across the river. Within a couple of days I was fully wired and good to go. I bought new leisure batteries, swapped out all my lights for LED bulbs, got a 12V adapter for my laptop, and after that never needed to run the engine to charge the batteries again. My single solar panel would go on to provide enough energy for everything I needed, apart from a power-thirsty fridge and a washing machine, which I'd have to carry on without.

I was starting to feel like a proper boater, part of a spirited, admirable and resilient community of people recognisable by the cork balls on keys hung from pockets and a sneaky engine oil stain on skin or clothing. We were not sailors or fishermen, we did not boat on open seas or around coasts under big beautiful sails in a sea breeze. We chugged noisily along skinny inland city channels on waters not blue, but black, green and with a rainbow of oil. We were more crust than salt. Many boaters were on the water through a desire for freedom – freedom to move, freedom from the trappings of full-time employment, freedom to be creative. Some wanted a life fuller, wilder, more adventurous. Some were lost and with nowhere else to go. Some all of the above. They were lawyers, doctors, journalists, musicians, carpenters, poets, makers, architects, space scientists. Their floating homes were all as unique as their proud owners. They had required days, months, sometimes years of work, and both emotional and financial investment. Unlike the flats which we'd often moor alongside, which came fully modernised, fitted out and ready to go, boats were often semi- and sometimes fully self-built. We were our own architects, adapting our living space to suit us. Our homes also extended beyond the boat's walls, with surroundings playing just as important a part. We turned them around to get a sunnier front deck, shuffled them along to be closer to a friend, cruised them further upstream to be closer to the wider stretch of grass or to a quieter spot if we needed to hide away, adjusted ropes to be able to see the moon through the bedroom window at night. Our space shifted with the weather and with each fortnightly move. Our portable homes did not need to comply with building regulations, they were multiple nests in a rookery, formation unplanned.

This shifting cluster of floating homes moved flock-like, if slowly. Like all unofficial settlements, it had formed organically. Residing on the periphery, it was a self-built, fluid village upon waterways once shunned and undesirable. We shared these edges, these beautiful often-overlooked boundaries, with other marginalised communities and secluded societies; out-of-sight travellers whose permanent sites lay behind riverside hedgerows, the unwatched homeless who pitched tents amongst the bushes and beneath overlooked bridges, addicts able to freely feed their habits, groups of eastern European men who sat on benches waiting hopefully for work.

Gradually that second summer I started to cross paths more often with the same people, and they became close friends. I first met Tommy early one June morning when I was standing on deck to feel the rising sun on my skin. Later in the day the towpath would be filled with life: boaters fixing boats, cats hopping between rooftops, nomadic kids pottering about on small wooden bikes, bundles of big dogs and their tired owners with half-empty beers in hand. But in the early hours, it was quiet. All mine. My ears pricked. *Queep queep queep.* A noisy red-headed fuzzy coot chick who liked exploring had ventured too far from his nest. From dawn till dusk, Mama and Papa coot searched for plastics and twine, diving in the green swampy water, picking up twigs and rubbish before taking breaks on a nearby half-sunken row boat. My neighbour Tommy, who I'd soon learn was a cocktail king and lover of wildlife, was also watching the chick from his side hatch. Tommy was larger than life and looked sturdy. His ear-length fluffy strawberry-blond hair reminded me of rolled hay bales. His sunburnt nose blushed beneath oversized glasses, and the top buttons of his untucked short-sleeved Hawaiian shirt were left undone.

"Cheeky chicky! Fucking noisy thing. Gotta love him. Ah, chicky. He's been on his own little missions this morning he has. Fucking little chicky."

"Morning," I replied, giving him a wave. Looking at Tommy, stubbled and rosy like a Somerset cider brewer, swearwords flowing from his mouth in a thick South London accent followed by thoughtful words on wildlife, it was impossible to imagine him high up in one of Canary Wharf's banking towers managing IT systems – but that, I'd later learn, was his job.

My kettle began to whistle.

"Right, I'm going to make a cup of tea and get on with some work. Nice meeting you, neighbour. I'm Danie."

"Tommy. My bird's called Becky."

"I look forward to meeting her. What's your boat called?"

"*Phoenix.*"

"*Genesis.*"

"Nice. See ya, Danie girl."

Tommy would be there for me during future scrapes. Like the time *Genesis* got stuck in the mud in the middle of the cut in Tottenham, north London. I heaved with all my strength on a barge pole dug into the sludge beneath to try to free her.

Twenty minutes passed, and still, I was marooned. Slowly, a twenty-strong gang of North London swans surrounded me, big blobs of brilliant white feathers floating like islands. They seemed savvy, angsty, patrolling their skinny patch of territory.

Eventually, a bloke walking along the towpath asked if he could help. "Can you see if anyone's in on one of those boats up there, and ask if they can give me a nudge or tow?" I asked him, and he obligingly set off in search of help. But he returned alone, shaking his head. *Damn.* I racked my brain. *Who do I know nearby?* I remembered that I'd seen Tommy's boat *Phoenix* moored not too far away. Pulling the stop to kill the noisy engine, I dialled his number.

"Danie girl," he answered, full of energy.

"Tommy, I'm stuck in the mud, are you in?"

"Ah, no mate, shit, you got a barge pole?" he said, his voice brash and comforting.

"Yeah, I've tried that. I'm fully lodged."

"Give the engine some revs in reverse, try and blast a channel in the silt. Otherwise you might have to wait for a boat to come along and pull you out. Sorry, mate. If you ever need a hand another time or get stuck, just give me a call yeah?"

"Thanks, Tommy."

"Good luck."

Tommy did not sugar coat things. He was a grafter, often inappropriately comedic, and his well-placed heart held some secret battle wounds. Behind his joker exterior there was father-like maturity, and I knew after this phone call he was the person I could call if I was in trouble, that in an emergency, he'd have the right advice.

What now? I stood still. Stranded. Then, a gust of wind swept round the bend. I felt *Genesis* shifting. This was it, engine on, throttle into gear, revs, muddied water fountaining behind. She was going, she was going, and with the next gust I was free.

Boat and towpath gatherings were raucous, raw and rosy-cheeked. Boaters knew how to party. I knew this from my first summer. Seemingly calm waters held a lively undercurrent, and that second summer I couldn't help but get swirled up in the ebullient swoosh of it all again. Like the time, Holly and I stumbled upon a watery wedding. It was dusk on a Saturday night, and the city's sounds were dimming. I was moored in Haggerston but that afternoon Holly and I had wandered the towpath and found ourselves in Hackney Wick, where graffiti decorated the locks, pubs spilled out onto the towpath and half-constructed buildings stood with glass yet to be fitted in the empty window frames. In the lingering warmth of summer, Holly and I decided to explore. I sang as we walked along the towpath which glistened as the last glimmers of evening sun caught the puddles that remained from a downpour in the morning. Did the city get prettier the closer you lived to the canal, I wondered? Or did living on the water open your eyes to more beauty within the city grey? We veered off the towpath into a maze of East London's canal-side warehouses. Tattooed artists and girls with cool hair roamed. This was the Mecca for creative, alternative twenty-somethings. In the concrete yard of a warehouse, a bonfire was burning, mesmerising and drawing in people, including us, like moths to a light bulb. We stood around its warmth with a young drag queen, and people dressed in a mixture of pyjamas, sequinned tops, and colourful leggings. Just beyond the glow, a speedboat was tied to the water's edge, and before I knew what was going on we all piled in. Within moments Holly and I were whizzing along the mucky cut past the Olympic Park. There were holes in the boat filled with expanding foam just below where we were sitting, and the weight of us and the other people aboard lowered the boat so that the water was barely an inch away from spilling over the sides and quickly sinking us.

The little speedboat turned off the Lea and onto the Hertford Cut alongside Victoria Park. We clambered out at the bottom lock like glittery pirates. On the dark, heavy water, I could see multiple narrowboats tied side by side to each other, creating a raft taking up the width of the canal and blocking navigation. Silhouettes of figures on the boat roofs danced to heavy bass and amplified instruments. Fairy lights were draped from makeshift masts, and bodies hopped across rooftops. In the coming years, towers of glossy, expensive apartments would be built by this lock, and a late-night bar would draw in crowds, but back then, before the developers swooped and took this patch for themselves, it was a dark and empty stretch, with unlit bridges and nothing but a small Garden Centre two locks up. Except for some boaters welding on the empty towpath, scorching sparks spitting in glittery arcs, there was no one. It was lawless.

Holly was drunk and her legs began to wobble. I tried to keep her up as we crossed over the lock. Then, coming towards us, I saw a beautiful barefoot bride. It was Jess, who I'd met a few times on the canal. She looked like a dream. Long, blond, wavy hair down to her waist, a slim-fitting ivory silk dress on her delicate frame and a crown of white and purple wild flowers. She had more on her mind than the fact that we had just accidentally crashed her wedding party. Her new mother-in-law had just moments before slipped between boats and possibly broken her collarbone, and Jess was desperately weaving between the moving bodies to find the paramedic. A barge wheelhouse roof which people were dancing on had also collapsed. I turned back to where Holly had been standing just moments before, but she was gone. My surroundings moved in slow motion around me as I scanned the scene for a glimpse of her. Dazed eyes caught mine, dancing bodies swirled, as I looked for Holly's tracks in between fuzzy fairy lights, as if she were a rare wild creature that I must protect. I noticed there was glass broken on the floor by my sandalled feet. I was getting worried. Then, I spotted her, with Jazzy Steve, who'd propped Holly on the top of one of the narrowboats. She was sitting with legs dangling over the side, swaying, doll-like, moments away from falling in and being crushed. "Get her down!" I shouted, so my voice would be heard over the music. It wasn't. I pushed through the crowd and took as much of her weight as I could to get her down. We hobbled back over the lock in a strange four-footed totter. It was time to go home. From the snug safety of *Genesis* later, it almost seemed as if the wedding party had been a mirage in the dark night.

Life on the canal, to the daytime stroller, looked calm. But I was now beneath its surface, discovering that when the sun sets and the crowds leave, swells of unseen currents could catch you by surprise. That at night, these city waterways became anything but tranquil. Slivers of urban wild became wilder. Under the cover of darkness, illegal raves were set up in riverside marshlands, nomads partied deep within tunnels, and lovers were married atop the roofs of boats.

Holly left the city not long after that night. Without much warning, she found a job up north to be closer to where her family lived, after struggling to pick up work which paid enough to afford to live in London. I was happy for her, but sad to say goodbye to my friend who had given me such moral support.

Winter was approaching, sneaking up as it had last year. Throughout summer, the approaching winter was unimaginable. I hadn't thought about the nearing dark evenings, how before long I would be lugging coal and opening locks in the cold rain. The six months of daily fires were soon to begin and boat life was that little bit harder again. But even though Holly had left, I wasn't alone; I now knew more people on the water and close friendships were forming.

Sam, the neurologist I had met during my first summer on the water, came to my rescue one autumn evening. I was struggling to close the rusted lock around my bike wheel and the steel bar on the roof of the boat, when I heard someone shout "Hi!"

I looked up to see two guys I didn't recognise who seemed drunk. I ignored their call.

"So rude. Why don't you say 'hi' back? Arrogant!" one of them yelled. I stood up on the roof and turned to look at them. They had now stopped walking and were just standing outside my home, staring at me. "I don't know who you are," I said, scowling. I wasn't in the mood for whatever they wanted to talk about.

"You *will* know who I am by the end of tonight, love," one replied, catching my eyes before laughing and staggering south towards Hackney Wick, turning back once more to shout the name of my boat, "*Genesis.*"

My nerves shaken, I decided to move the boat. Engine on, brass pin through the tiller, cast off the lines. I cruised upstream a little, ignoring a few mooring spaces even though I knew *Genesis* would fit, just to get further away. To my relief I spotted a dark-green boat I was familiar with, Sam's boat *Madame George*. I double-moored next to him, tying the ropes across the bow and stern of his boat onto the bank, so the two men wouldn't be able see the big swirly *Genesis* on the side of my boat if they came back. I was blocking Sam's view of the water, but he didn't mind.

"Don't worry," he reassured me. "They will have forgotten all about what they said by tonight."

Until now, I'd been cruising entirely solo, flitting between groups of people for two-week stints. There had been neighbours I passed many times, some I had to leave behind and never saw again. But from now on, one neighbour would remain constant. Sam and I began cruising together, moving our boats to the same area and mooring up next to each other. It was the start of what would become a bigger group of friends, each of them bursting with life, who would move boats in convoy. It was the beginning of my floating family, the flotilla.

7

My arm was covered in soot as I lay on my side, reaching up. My bare legs, awkwardly curled beneath me, were becoming tingly with pins and needles. Laboriously I scraped ash down from the chimney flue, onto the fire plate and then into the stove with my hand. Mango, muddy-pawed and watching me with long lashes, was curled and wet from his walk. The lingering smell of damp dog filled my small boat. It was the turn of a new season. The temperature had fallen, the trees bore few leaves, and the condensation had arrived. In the short space of a year and a half, life had become cyclical. I knew winter was near and so it was time to sweep the chimney, and begin battening down the hatches. Soon, boat roofs would become well stocked with wood, kindling and coal. Inside space would become more compact, with kindling stacked near the stove (but not too close), an extra duvet on the bed and big warm coats and scarves by the door. Chimneys would chug continuously, and dog walks were to be in the dark for months. Sleep would be in thermals and hugging a hot-water bottle. Skies would look larger, evening light would be lower, underfoot soggier. Gathered around wood burners we boaters would begin planning the next year's craning, blacking, repainting. Whilst landlubbers grew sluggish, we'd still be out battling the wind and rain, lifting sacks of coal down from roof tops. The hardest season was on its way, but we'd not be hibernating through the red berries and crisp days. We'd feel the harsh bite of the cold; hear the dull sound of frosty mornings. We'd spend nights euphorically warm and see skies full of winter glitter.

"Camden Lock will be closed for maintenance works over winter." Word spreads fast on the canal. Boaters would now have to choose which side of Camden Lock, in north London near Regent's Park, they wanted to stay on until spring. To the east was King's Cross, Angel, Hackney, Tottenham and beyond, to the West was Paddington, Little Venice, Kensal Green and beyond. The weekend before the stoppage, everyone was on the move, heading east or west, where they'd be stuck for the next few months. Winter towpath moorings were available this year, where you could pay a few hundred quid for the privilege of being able to stay in one place and not have to move every two weeks except for going to collect water and emptying the loo. It was an attractive option, especially during the coldest months. After this year, winter moorings wouldn't be available in greater London again. And so, for the first time in eighteen months, I decided to stay still for a short while and enjoy the luxury of a neighbourhood, routine and permanence. Sam and I, and a few others, would be spending the winter in Hackney Wick.

On the day before the lock closed, queues at the taps were four boats, and four hours, long. Not everyone made it before the closure in Camden. Sam's sister Alice, a nurse for the homeless, and her carpenter boyfriend Ben, who were new on the water and lived aboard their boat *Genevieve*, were left on the other side. They had to wait for the season to pass, and the repairs to the ancient locks to be done, before they could join us.

As I slowly edged *Genesis* into the Wick, my ears flooded

with the sounds of buildings coming down and going up. The area's roughness, which I once loved, was now being tidied up. The secret wonders and unclaimed, unmanaged landscapes I'd stumbled across just a year before were now signposted and manicured. The spectacular view of London's skyline that I'd discovered last winter, with its dense layers of cranes and towers, had gone with the removal of a footbridge that connected the platforms at Hackney Wick station. Gone with the regeneration and consequent gentrification, never to be seen again. Money had moved there, and fast. In an area changing so quickly, those who used to call it home couldn't keep up. Artists and families were being forced out by the rapidly rising rents. Buildings along the river that were once squatted were being transformed into million-pound apartments before your eyes, like a high-speed time-lapse. The Wick's once-affordable workspaces had turned into gated communities. Spray-painted on a makeshift wall: 'I CAME. I SAW. I TRIED MDMA. MY PARENTS BOUGHT A FLAT'

Sam and I chose our winter residence for the next few months: a familiar spot next to the footbridge to Fish Island on the Hertford Union canal, also called Duckett's canal after the man who built it to try and save time by not having to go all the way to Limehouse to join the Regent's. There was a gap for Sam to fit his boat next to mine.

And so there we were, on our boats, separated from these pricey postcodes by just a sliver of water.

The sound of heavy footsteps walking over my roof thundered above my bed, back and forth, back and forth. I sat bolt upright in bed. I had no idea if I'd just fallen asleep or if it was the early hours of the morning. Men's voices accompanied the stomping, along with a rattling engine and loud music. Another person walked along my gunwales, rocking *Genesis* furiously. Ropes were being tied. I could hear everything through the thin steel shell of my bedroom. I peered out and could see that it was a large barge with a tall mast that had just crunched along the side of my *Genesis*. Suddenly furious, I stormed out into the dark in pyjamas.

"What the fuck?" I yelled. "It's the middle of the night! You just hit my boat?"

Their replies came mumbled – half sheepish, half bravado-laden excuses as to what had happened. I realised that they were about my age, in their mid- to late-twenties, and they were stinking drunk. This was not the last time this would happen.

In the boating community, it's considered friendly to say hello to your neighbour if you plan to double-moor alongside them, maybe an introduction, checking it's alright, and perhaps even a cup of tea or a whisky or rum. Generally, boaters also stick to the canal etiquette of turning off their engines and generators between 8pm and 8am. If someone does cruise through the night and finds they have to double-moor, generally they do so as quietly as possible. But booze had got the better of these pirates. After I realised it was pointless to pull them up on their bad boat handling and lack of neighbourliness, I said goodnight and went back inside to bed.

As I lay there, the face from my past appeared in my mind again. It often happened when I woke in the night, or when I was moored somewhere that made me feel frightened. Memories of *him* would flood me. *Go away,* I said in my head, as a tear fell down my cheek, *Go away.*

I closed the front door and the curtains, even though it was sunny outside. It was morning, and Jake had arrived on *Genesis* like I'd asked him to. The night before I'd decided to dig out the 12V TV which came with the boat from beneath my bed and watch something for the first time in two years. It was late, but I didn't want to sleep yet. The first thing that came on was a TV show presented by a radio presenter who had sexually assaulted me some years before. We'd met as I was waiting to do a voice-over. He asked me out for lunch at the weekend, and despite my flatmate at the time saying it seemed a bit weird that he wanted to meet at his house, I went. When I arrived, instead of heading out for lunch, he invited me inside and upstairs. I was young, and didn't want to seem rude. The next part happened very quickly. I ended up having to physically wrestle him to tear the condom which he'd quickly taken out of its packet out of his hands so he wouldn't have sex with me. He told me it would just be quick. He was smiling, and acting like this wrestle was a fun game. I used all my strength to get the condom off him before he managed to put it on, my heart pounding as I pretended to giggle so as to keep what was happening from turning worse. I got it, and split it with my nails. It was his last one. I then allowed him to touch me. I couldn't think of how else to get out of the situation. He fell asleep, and I snuck out of his room and house. And now, there he was, surrounded by a crowd of screaming fans. I froze, watching his face on the glowing screen, his face inside my boat. After a couple of minutes, I turned the TV off, put it back under my bed, and sat back on the sofa. Shock simmered, and I was left silent, angry. Nothing had happened after the assault. Luckily, I had been able to tell a friend straight away and, wanting to forget about it and avoid any further ordeal, I had let it go. I hadn't bumped into the man again. But seeing him grinning on a TV screen triggered a different, more painful memory. I felt a surge of determination bubble up. My

113

anger made me courageous. I knew in that moment that I had to tell Jake what I hadn't ever been able to talk to anyone about before, what had happened to me when I was a young teenager. I texted Jake, asking him to come over in the morning, and went to sleep.

Jake arrived on my boat early, ready to hear me talk, but during the night my bravery had wobbled, and now my lips couldn't find the words. *Will I ever be able to say it? Where do I begin? What will he say?* All the worries that had muzzled me before made me mute again. My eyes filled with tears. It was the hardest thing I'd ever tried to do.

"There isn't anything you could say that would ever change how I feel about you," said Jake. "Just start anywhere, you're safe," he reassured me.

I could barely breathe. Thirteen years had passed, but it felt like yesterday. I sat on Jake's lap, on my little sofa-bed made of odd-sized wooden slats with exposed screws and an ever-changing cover of throws, blankets and patterned sheets.

The morning went by, and still I was wordless. Mango, now definitely too big to fit on the top step by the front door, patiently waited and wondered why we weren't doing anything. He tried to awkwardly nap with his legs dangling off the step, waking up from time to time to readjust so as not to slip off. My eyes were puffed red, my brow tense. Throwing myself off a cliff would have been easier.

"You could just start saying any words," he said. "Even if they are wrong and don't come out right, it doesn't matter, they don't have to be in the right order."

It was the first proper party I'd been to, in the church hall where I'd gone to Brownies. I was fourteen, wearing a top

I'd borrowed from a girl at school who had going-out kind of clothes. Normally, my school friends and I would have sleepovers, make up dance routines, practise singing songs, talk about the boys we fancied in class. But now we were at a proper party, and older kids were smoking and drinking in the toilets. When the party was over, we ended up in a park nearby with the boy my friend fancied. He was in the year above and was with his older friends from a different school who we didn't know. One of them asked for my number. We'd all just got our first mobile phones, and he texted me the next day arranging to meet up. I knew Mum would be on a late shift, and I'd be home alone, so I said he could come over. He arrived on his bike and brought a friend with him. The boy's friend – tall, slim, blue eyes and light-brown hair, wearing a hoody – waited in my brother's room next door while the boy and I kissed in my room. We sat on the futon beneath my single, high bunk bed under glow-in-the-dark-stars. It was a small room, with just enough space for a desk; I'd hang my clothes in the airing cupboard in the corridor. Everything was multi-coloured, and decorated with dream-catchers, fairy lights, toys and photos in glittery frames. The boy had both his ears pierced, wore a white sports top, a cap and a gold chain round his neck. They both left at 9.45pm, fifteen minutes before I knew Mum would get home from work.

Later that night I got a text from the boy's friend. He told me he liked me, or something like that. I don't know how he got my number. I don't remember how it all began, when it was that I first went to his house on a council estate after school. I don't remember what he said that made me not tell anyone else where I was going or who I was going to meet. But I can still walk it in my head. Through town, past the shops, up a sloped, thin road that was always in shadow, past the phone box, turn right. It was kind of exciting. The sun was shining, and a boy fancied me. It was something to do, somewhere to go. At home there were lots of arguments. When I arrived at the boy's house, still in my school uniform, his dad turned to him and said, "Is this your Tuesday girl?" I didn't know what he meant and just smiled. The boy led me straight upstairs into his bedroom.

Inside, the walls were covered in pictures of semi-naked hairless women in all sorts of poses. Tens of posters and pages from magazines. I'd never seen pictures like that before. Maybe I'm meant to look like them, I thought. We sat on his bed. He was seventeen, and worked in the fishmonger's. He played basketball. He had a moped. I was fourteen, barely developed, weighed about seven stone, and was wearing my first ever bra, which I didn't need, but the other girls were wearing them so I wanted one. He had a smell. Unwashed testosterone. He was tall, lean with wide shoulders. Before I knew it, he somehow silently hollowed me out from my clothing, excavating me like a magic trick, unbuckling and un-buttoning. I lay there letting it happen, letting him have unrestricted access to me, letting him have sex with me. He told me he liked his chest kissed. I can remember the taste. I was silent, complying. I didn't want this, but he looked happy. He knew what to do, he was in control of this, he moved me around. He came inside me. Then gave me a hug. In exchange for my body, doing what he wanted, I got a hug. We watched part of a movie together on the telly he had in his room, *American Pie*. Not all of the movie, just a bit. That part, lying together for half an hour, that small amount of affection which came after he took me, was what would make me come back again. I was desperate for love. He took me home on the back of his moped, back to Mum's before she got home. A spare helmet just for me. I wrapped my arms tightly around his waist from behind, my face pressed against his back. I didn't tell anyone. For some reason, it was a secret. In my bed, disorientated, his smell and stickiness on me, I felt like

116

I couldn't see properly, like when you step indoors after being in the sun and things slowly come into focus.

I went back again. And again. And again. It didn't hurt, it wasn't violent, and so I could not see with my young eyes his coercion, his grooming. I couldn't see what was happening, how obviously vulnerable I was, how clever he was at exploiting that. I would do whatever he wanted. "It's what you do when you really like someone," he would tell me, and I believed him. And with those words I'd submit to his persuasion. Usually he would have sex with me from behind. When he came I would be looking at a wall, no face. Sometimes he would hold my hair and gently lead my head down his body and hold it there until he came so I would have to swallow it. Afterwards, once he'd finished and another piece of me was taken, I would lie confused. But I was with someone, I was somewhere, his arm was around me and *American Pie* was on his TV. This bit felt nice, normal. I would wonder, was I meant to enjoy it? Why weren't we girlfriend and boyfriend? Why didn't the rest of it, the most of it feel nice? Why didn't I feel right? I tried to ask if we could go out, but he already had a girlfriend who lived at the top of the street, a bit older than me. He said she wouldn't sleep with him until she was sixteen. Young and with no real relationship experience, I accepted this. Then I began not to like myself. I started believing that this was all I was good for, all I was wanted for. My mind started becoming more and more detached from my body, and my happy self became more upset, the feeling of not being able to see worsened, and the arguments with my mum got far worse. At school I acted as if nothing was happening, and avoided doing anything about it. That was the best I could do.

He was not fazed by any risk of pregnancy, and only sometimes used a condom, so there were times I had to take the morning-after pill. We had been taught about sexually transmitted infections at school, and so I went to the hospital by myself, and asked where to go to get a test. I waited in a room, and then lay on a bed with a paper roll along it, with my little legs held up in stirrups, feeling cold metal and then a swab pushed up inside me whilst a strange woman who didn't like me kept telling me to relax, getting annoyed that I was tense. More things in me that I didn't want. Afterwards I sat on a bench outside the hospital trying to stop crying so I could get on the bus home. A kind nurse saw me and asked what was wrong, but I couldn't tell her. I didn't know how to. I had no one to tell when I got the results back; I got the all-clear.

I began not to care about myself; his violation had destroyed my sense of self-worth. Sometimes he would text me asking for sex and I, killing time and wandering around, would go to him. Sometimes it happened in the woods, sometimes in his room, sometimes in the caravan parked outside his house. I wasn't ready for any of this. But it was happening. He didn't meet any of my friends, or my family.

One day, when all of this was happening, a girl even younger than me who lived near him and must have seen me coming and going, came up to me and told me that he'd raped her in the caravan, that he'd had a knife, that she'd bled. I can't remember whether the blood was because she'd lost her virginity or if he'd cut her. She told me she'd told the police, and asked if I would speak to them about him, tell them about him. I called him. I screamed and screamed at him. I was hysterical. I begged him to tell me what happened. He told me he didn't do it. I wanted to believe him, and so I convinced myself I did. The police came to the skinny house, explained to my mum that they needed me to go to the police station and give a video statement about a man I knew who had been arrested for rape. In the video interview, the police wanted details, how did I know him, what do I know about him, what was my connection to him, anything, any details at all. I told them nothing. I had no words. I didn't understand what had been happening. I hadn't even told a friend, how could I tell a police officer? I had gone to his house. I hadn't said no (not the same thing as giving consent, but I didn't know that). I was gross, I thought. The only thing I said was, "I can't tell you anything he has done to me, but I can tell you he is a bad person." I don't know what happened after that, what the police did, what happened to that girl.

None of my friends were having sex. No one knew this boy, the seventeen-year-old fishmonger, who had gone to a school I knew no one at, who lived in a council estate I had never been to before. No one would understand. Even I didn't understand. I started to cry a lot. I would wander around the park at night and cry. I realised I had to make it stop. I wrote him a long letter explaining that I wanted everything to end. I spent a long time writing it and built myself up to reading it to him after school. We arranged to meet on the top of a hill surrounded by woodland overlooking my town and my old primary school. Sitting by a tree, I read the letter out loud. The paper was trembling. When I finished reading my letter and looked up, he kissed me, and raped me again. I silently cried as he manoeuvred me. I stared at the tree in front of me, and then I could see myself with him from behind but from above. I left my body completely.

I ran home. In Ben's room there was our new computer which Mum had taken a loan out to pay for, because I'd told her everyone else at school had one. I typed what happened. I asked her to go in and read it. I waited outside the door. I think she wanted to talk about it, but I just wanted to call my friend and tell her to come over. Mum said my friend couldn't come, she wanted me to talk to her, to talk about what had happened. I didn't know how to. I got angry, and it somehow quickly turned into a big argument, as it often did.

Not long after, two of his friends took it in turns to have sex with me in the small woodland behind their estate, one after the other. I didn't realise that was why we had met there. I stood there with the two of them, and, when I realised what was happening, I walked into the trees and they followed. I was now conditioned to do something that gave me no pleasure because that was what was expected, and I didn't know how to stop it. My school tights got dirty and laddered, so I had to go home without them on.

I remember telling him about those two boys. He didn't care. I wanted him to care, I wanted to believe that this had all been love and not abuse. But it wasn't. I stopped going. It stopped. I had survived, but I was ashamed. I blamed myself. I didn't want anyone to know, believing they would think badly of me. I hadn't fought back, I thought. I just lay there. So what was that? It was confusing and upsetting and I could not, and would not, share my experience. I felt everything from numbness, to denial, to guilt, to embarrassment, to worthlessness, to depressed. I was alienated in my experience. I minimised, suppressed, disassociated, moved on. Almost immediately I was with a different boy, my first proper boyfriend. There was no time to process what had happened, what had now stopped happening. I was now spending every spare minute with this new, very sweet boyfriend, an apprentice mechanic, who told me he would definitely propose to me when we were older. He loved me. He bought me heart-shaped balloons. But as much as I wanted to quickly erase the memory of what had happened, and enjoy this first love, I was cut up. After sex I would immediately be in uncontrollable tears, zoned out, even though it was always consensual and loving. I would have to hide in a bathroom until the wave of overwhelming emotion passed. I thought I could leave what had happened in the past, forget it ever happened. I wanted to be fine, to be normal and

120

happy. But those suppressed memories were there. That trauma, violation, did happen, no matter how much I tried to pretend it hadn't.

A year or so after, I started to go to free counselling sessions at the YMCA. I think I went there for a few months, sitting in a portacabin with a really nice lady who had a blanket and a little electric heater. I never told her what happened, I just talked a bit about my mum, my dad, home life. I constantly skirted around the subject. I used to lose track of what day it was then and missed my final session and never got to thank her. I had planned to bring her flowers. My friends mostly stayed on at sixth form, but I went to college, a new start. I got a new boyfriend, new friends, I thought it was all left in the past. I lost touch with my school friends, but I was having fun. I was studying Photography, Performing Arts, Media and Sociology, and doing OK. But I hadn't escaped him. When I was seventeen and at college, a girl came up to me in the smoking area and told me she had found lots of photos of young girls in underwear on the phone of a man she had started seeing. The man was him and one of the photos was of me. She seemed a little worried and thought I should know. I never saw him take a photo of me. *What is he going to do with a photo of me? What if my new boyfriend finds out, what will he think of me, what if he breaks up with me?* He didn't find out about him, but he did find out about the two friends in the woods and asked me about it. I was uncontrollable, screaming and sobbing and angry and upset, telling him I couldn't explain but to please believe me, that what he had heard wasn't how it was. He didn't leave me, and I forced myself to forget about it. I was getting on with life now, I was fine.

Time had stopped.

Jake was still there. He was still holding me. I was still in my boat, un-sunk.

"I love you," Jake said, without a fraction of hesitation. "I love and admire you even more than I did before. I'm so, so glad you made it to me." He hugged me so tight. I stared at him. I was floating. Light. It had halved in weight.

Before this day, immediately after blissful moments with Jake, sometimes my perfect present would trigger the painful past, and suddenly, without any warning, I would be filled with panic, sadness and shame. I would, in an instant, be terrified, vulnerable, not in my room, but in *his* room, tears welling up, a knot in my throat. This intrusion was like a freak flood, an unexpected tsunami, and there was nothing I could do to stop it. It wasn't detailed specific memories that were rushing in, but an uncontrollable and overwhelming re-experiencing of emotions I'd felt before, when I was fourteen. I would quickly try to bring myself back into the room. I would make sure I could see Jake's face, wiggle my toes, move my fingers, go and splash my face, and it would pass. But after sharing my secret, these flashbacks, these rushes of overwhelming and debilitating emotion, didn't happen like they had before. I was free.

When spring came, it was heady, the weather endlessly changeable. The sky would sporadically darken as the wind picked up, and I'd know that a downpour was imminent. On the morning I steered *Genesis* north up the River Lea, low, dark-grey nimbostratus clouds – thick enough to block the sun – burst and drenched me. The rain smelled of stone. My mind was not on London, work, decisions, but on lining up my boat to go through the centre of a small old bridge, built in a time when traffic was a horse and cart. The wet weather left me feeling euphoric, almost triumphant, and part of the outside world. I buzzed in the wet, high on endorphins and dopamine from the physical activity, fresh air and natural light. Soon the sky cleared, leaving behind fluffy, splodgy cumulus and sunshine.

On these spring mornings, birdsong out-noised the city traffic at daybreak. The *chip chip* of the chaffinch, loud slow *chik chik chik* of the blackbird, and flutey *tsip* of the song thrush, culminated in an April crescendo of sweet sound, which washed over me like a baptism. I was beginning to recognise the sounds of each bird. Soon the river birds would begin nest-building, and I would watch them get feistier as they defended their home and their young and protected their claims by chasing off other waterfowl.

Grasslands were bouncing back and glistening with dew, and the ancient meadow hedgerows that line the banks of narrow winding ribbons of river were coming alive. The daffodils looked quite at home in the cool blustery sunshine. Purple crocuses were cropping up too, and white blossoms with butter-yellow centres had begun opening on the twiggy trees. I spied a type of dandelion I'd never seen before: larger, fluffier, its stems exploding into a firework of colour. The daisies were lazier than the buttercups, and only opened after a long lie-in in the morning, protecting their pollen from the morning's dampness. *Soon,* I thought to myself, *I will be warm. Grow spring, grow.*

Sam and I moored near the large, boggy expanse of flat green that is the Walthamstow Marshes, a Site of Special Scientific Interest, nestled away from the grey urban surroundings. "The Magic Bend" we'd later call that spot – a sweeping curve of river where the skies were big and a spectacle. We were close to Springfield Marina where we could pick up gas and chemical toilet blue. The people there had permanent moorings for their boats, and tended to take their boats out for a week or two's holiday or a day trip a few times a year when the sun shone. These boaters were of a different tribe. Their homes clean, their inner workings not as well known and engine rooms less frequented. They didn't tend to have conversations about which locks were stiff, which bins had been removed, where hidden taps were to be found. Shoreline power and a permanent mooring kept them more attached to the world on land. They had electric toasters, unlimited water supply, washing machines on site. There was an island in the middle of the boats that was home to a kingfisher, nesting swans and a heron. Noisy, exotic green, ring-neck parakeets scored the sky above with flashes of lime; once domesticated birds, now flying wild and free. Sometimes I envied these boaters. But right now, with the new spring, I was content with what I had.

With the new location came a new makeshift office to write my TV continuity scripts in, a buzzy little café by the rowing club where the brunches were good and cheap. The water was not just used by boaters, but rowers too. In light, slender, streamlined crafts they were raring, pumped, precise, pulling back in straight lines and travelling with purpose. They sliced the stillness of the river in perfect unison, in perfect repetition. My route to work now took me over the footbridge that crossed the Navigation, along a potted puddly towpath, past the Beam Engine Museum, which contains a very old and enormous engine originally built to pump sewage from Tottenham to Europe's largest treatment works in Beckton. Then I'd pass through the back of a warehouse that used to be a timber wharf where exotic woods were brought up from Limehouse on Thames barges. Old industrial cranes arched over the water, home to many a perching black cormorant, wings spread and drying out. They'd stand, dinosaur-like, with black scaly wings glinting with green and indigo, their long, primitive necks outstretched and covered in partially waterproof plumage. Flocks of other wild birds flew overhead towards the wetlands on the other side of the river. I'd pass men fishing optimistically for who knows what, as ducks made crisscross patterns in the water, and crows walked over the newly cut grass. Soon I'd be in Stamford Hill, surrounded by Orthodox Jewish mothers dressed in black with matching bobs, pushing large prams, their husbands in traditional Hasidic hats and small glasses shepherding large packs of quiet children in matching outfits.

One Sunday I walked along the river's marshy edge, boggy soil sucking at my feet. As I walked, the tension in my muscles relaxed and my hammering heart slowed. Instead of fogging my mind, the city's sounds became muffled, so I could see more clearly. Mango stopped and turned to check whether he could go ahead. "OK boy". He knew which way to go. I sat down, hidden amongst the grasses of Walthamstow Marshes, which towered above my head. I was surrounded by green and tucked just beyond the river. I had become a fox. Stealthy, hidden, soft-footed, watching people from a distance. I breathed in the grassy air, smiled, then breathed out. Mango was sitting beside me, my fox cub, the two of us immersed in nature. Mango had helped me to explore so many hidden paths and pockets of wild in London. He'd got me outdoors for hours every day, wandering paths unknown in the semi-wild landscape of the city's backyard, connecting me to the outside, and giving me a sense of purpose and responsibility. I felt feral. Like the edge-land I was in. The traffic-dodging, crowd-weaving, continuous sounds of the city, the constant barrage of stuff that demanded my attention and overwhelmed me was a million miles away. Here, in my wild, grassy labyrinth out of the city's sight, I felt balanced. The place helped me understand the secret I had told. The green and the water rinsed it away as if it were a grass stain on a dress.

On the canal, serendipitous chats with new and interesting neighbours were a constant occurrence. There was no way of knowing whether that week's lovely neighbour would become a life-long friend, be someone I would bump into on the towpath from time to time, or someone I would never see again. First meetings would happen so frequently that it was sometimes hard to remember them. But I remember meeting Abbie for the first time around this third spring, two years into my journey. It was at a towpath supper. She had marinated an entire celeriac and put it on the barbecue. There were also whole leeks cooking over the coals, spicy corn-on-the-cob and roasted red peppers stuffed with dhal. A small group of boaters had gathered, including a couple living in the next boat along who were documentary makers just back from Russia where they'd been undercover reporting on extreme levels of pollution. They told tales of how they'd been forced to spend each night backing up all their footage on secretly stashed hard drives in case they were caught. Sam introduced me to Abbie. He had met her at a hospital training day – she was a doctor too – and had discovered that not only did she live on a boat, but her boat, *Luna*, was moored nearby.

"I've just started cruising," she told us as we all sat on blankets sprawled across the towpath, bowls of food in hand. I had so far met a lot of men and couples on boats. Abbie was the first woman I had met who was also continuously cruising solo. She was beaming with life. Her eyes were decorated with glitter and she smiled as she spoke. She was taller than me, with a beautiful womanly figure. She was dressed in timeless floaty florals with her wavy long blonde hair half-pinned up. She was at the top of her profession. An ego-less career woman, solo boater and soon to become a sister to me, she was grounded and had the ability to breeze away worries.

I asked her which way she was heading.

"North up the Lea," she said. "Us too," I said. "We were thinking of mooring by Markfield Park, before Tottenham if you want to moor nearby?" In the coming weeks we moved our boats to the same places. We became a flotilla of three.

8

Jake, built for rainy seas and blustery mountains, was too hot and lying on the sofa inside the boat praying for a breeze to come through the open doors. I was soaking up every single ray of almost-summer sunshine I could out on the front deck, talking to fluffed-up cygnets and breathing in the long grass of the river bank. I was not long back after three weeks of walking high in the wilds of the Himalayas in Nepal with Jake's housemate. She and I had decided one night we needed to walk, and walk high, and had gone together. We trekked alone for eight hours a day and reached a mountain pass 5,416 meters above sea-level. Something I'm not sure I would have done if it wasn't for the boat. Then, the phone rang. It was Ben.

"Mum's in hospital. You need to get there quick. I've just arrived at Heathrow. I'll meet you there," he told me.

"What's happened?"

"She went back to the house. He was there."

"OK, I'm on my way," I said.

I turned to Jake. "We have to go right now. Mum's in hospital."

We jumped onto our bikes, I told Mango to heel, and we pedalled as fast as we could to Hackney Wick where, luckily, Jake's parents' car was parked because he was borrowing it. It took an hour to drive to the hospital. It was the same hospital where Mum had worked as an auxiliary nurse when I was a teenager.

As I rushed there, my mind churned through all the possible things that might have happened. I had thought Mum had reached a new, more positive stage of her life. Almost a year before she had finally summoned up the courage to leave the Wolf. After many near-escapes, where we'd thought we were getting her back and then didn't, she had finally done it. She had called me from her car. She was sobbing and sounded in shock, in disbelief.

"I've left, Danie," she said. "I just got in my car, and drove away. I've just pulled over." As she spoke, it was as if she was realising what she had done. "I didn't take anything with me. I… I just left."

"Keep driving, Mum, don't turn around, keep driving," I told her.

Since then, she'd been living in a secret safe place, an annex attached to another woman's house who let Mum stay there for a reduced rent in return for help with caring for her poorly husband. It was nice there. Mum had made it lovely by draping colourful fabrics over things, putting pictures of flowers up on the walls, and photos of Ben and me as little children on the fridge. She had her own little courtyard which she'd decorated with wind chimes and lanterns, and a greenhouse where she grew tomatoes. Mum was happy and safe. Ben and I could visit her, and the lady next door would let us stay in the spare room in her house. A few times Mum had come to stay with me on *Genesis*. She liked it, mostly. She'd help me with my herb and flower garden on the roof, make the boat look homely with more colour, and I'd make her a nice supper. But when she felt out of sorts, the constant whir of people past the windows and complete lack of privacy when on the front deck made her worse. She felt there was nowhere quiet to hide. She was right.

I arrived at the hospital to find Mum with her cheeks so swollen she was barely recognisable.

"Mum."

"Oh, Danie, you didn't need to come."

"What happened Mum, what happened?"

"I…" She struggled to answer my question. "I went back to the house."

"Why? You could have called me? I could have come with you."

"I wanted to get my things. I felt brave enough. I didn't think he'd be there."

"What did he do?"

"He lost it. He just… he just completely lost it. I thought he was going to really, really hurt me."

"Mum." I tried to imagine what it had been like. The Wolf was huge compared to my five-foot-tall mum and he had beaten her black and blue.

"All I could do was try and scratch him. I managed to, then when he saw blood on his arm he suddenly stopped and called the police."

"What?"

"He called the police and said I'd attacked him… Maybe he realised he'd gone too far and panicked? I don't know. The police came, saw me and arrested him straight away. An ambulance brought me here."

"Please, please don't ever go to that house again," I begged her.

"It's so weird," she said. "Now I can see it was all him all along, I can see who he truly is. He was never physically violent towards me, and so I thought it was all in my head. But now I know it was him who was not the normal one, not me."

It was hard for me to understand why my mum had stayed under the spell of the Wolf for so long, thinking that she was always the one in the wrong. But as I've now come to understand, it is common for women in controlling, abusive relationships to stay in them for many years for many different reasons; dependence on their partner, having nowhere to go, being overwhelmed, conflicting emotions, finding it difficult to make decisions, believing things will get better if they change their own behaviour. What had made it even harder for Mum, was the Wolf upsetting her mental wellbeing, sometimes setting off a collection of triggers which would rapidly stop her brain from working properly, before totally shutting her down. It sometimes left her unable to do anything, or to make the simplest of decisions. She would suddenly feel cut off from the world, and worthless. She told me that, when that happened, her brain would say to her, "Oh look, she's feeling a bit shit, let's kick her in the head and make her feel more shit." I imagined her head like a lock with the water gushing in through a broken sluice gate, uncontrollable, crashing against the sides and submerging her mind without warning, like a boat caught on the sill. But that day, when she could see the bruises on her own skin with her own eyes, not just silently feel them in her mind, she realised that she was the survivor, and he was the Wolf.

The hospital let us take Mum home. That evening, sitting beside her in her little courtyard where Ben, knowing that Mum always felt better when she was outside in the garden, had got her comfy and poured her a large glass of red wine, I prayed that this revelation would be a lasting one for my mum. That no man like the Wolf would take Mum again. For years whilst she was with him, Ben and I had worried about her. Sometimes everything would suddenly become very dramatic. We would be in a whir of panic and activity, throwing intense energy into helping. My desperate worry would turn me into a fierce protective mother of my own mum, and then everything would go quiet again. Mum would get better, and get on with her life.

There would be little conversation about it, no decompression, just me getting back to my life, Ben getting on with his and Mum getting on with hers. That was our coping mechanism. After the crazy ride, I'd go back to London, where everything had carried on as normal, and so I had to, too.

Before the boat, I would think, *who would understand? Who would want to talk about such sad things?* I'd only ever talked about my mum with my brother, and even then it was on a practical level, working out what we were going to do, or checking with each other if we'd heard from her. But on the boat, I told people. I had to: living so closely with other people it was impossible to hide how I was feeling. I would have to turn down boat suppers happening right next door because I was tired from coping with a crisis, and so had to tell people why. It surprised me how easy it was. And my friends understood. In fact, not only did they understand, but we talked about it, and they told me about their families, people they knew who had suffered from depression, or had gone through difficult times. For the first time, I had a support network beyond just my brother.

Out in the little courtyard in the garden, we all sat together in the night air surrounded by mum's twinkling lights and candles with the radio playing. Mum, despite her injuries and swollen face, was smiling and chatting, like she used to. Ben and I looked at each other. We'd got Mum back.

There was a day that spring when my legs buckled beneath me. A day when juggling the multitude of challenges that comes with being a solo female boater, living off-grid and nomadically, having a dog and a busy London freelance job all took its toll. I was walking home through Springfield Park in Upper Clapton overlooking the River Lea and Walthamstow Marshes. Blossom still lightly confettied the trees in delicate pink, peach and white, and dotting the ground were a few drooping stems of bold violet bluebells. Suddenly my legs gave way. It felt like they were filling up with lead and too heavy to stay straight. I was exhausted. It was only a two-mile walk home, but I wondered if I'd make it, it seemed impossible. For the first time, my usually reliable, strong body had said no. The coffee I'd drunk in the morning had long worn off and I was in trouble. A mum, holding the hands of her two young girls, spotted me as she walked past, looked back, and asked if I was OK. She didn't stop. I looked a state – hobbling, bent-kneed, with desperation and exhaustion etched on my face.

As I tried to walk on, I heard my name. "Danie? Are you OK?" I looked up to see a girl I had worked with a year or two before running across a road towards me. Tears began to roll down my face. "Sophie? I'm so tired. I'm trying to get home," is all I managed to get out. I was in a daze. I was so happy she was there. She put her arm around me to hold me up and made some jokes, perhaps so I wouldn't feel embarrassed about this strange situation. She walked me all the way back to the river and *Genesis*. Maybe my guardian angel had been looking out for me again, I thought.

Back on *Genesis*, I curled into a ball and wept. I didn't want to be hard up, like we had been growing up, I wanted to be financially stable for the children I wanted to have. I'd always promised myself I'd make everything wonderful when I had a family of my own, that if I worked really hard now I wouldn't have to work all the hours to cover the bills when I was a mum. I wanted to be able to provide stability, a home, a life without stress for my future children. I would get life right. This had, unwittingly, been my driving force, the core of everything I had been doing, the reason I was living in a floating steel box, saying yes to every job that came my way. Exhausted, I knew then that something had to change.

Life would be boring if it were easy, I thought as I sat on the bench on the hill in Springfield Park the next day. I had gone up there to walk Mango, but also because I knew there were important things to think about. The bench was tucked away in a pruned hedge, and the birds couldn't see me, so they flew low, skimming over my head. The sun began to set above the big fenced-off reservoir behind the river, creating a golden pink sky. I wasn't sure I could continue living the way I was for many months longer. Instead of becoming easier, the responsibility was becoming more overwhelming. As I sat there looking out onto the city, questions buzzed through my mind. Could I work less, make this life on the edge permanent? Or would I have to slip back into postcodes, electricity bills and the rat race? How could I gain more time – the modern luxury – in my life? I wondered whether I could forever be nomadic, or if I wanted, needed, to settle. I had put everything into this; if I gave up now, what would I have? I thought about how I could re-ballast, make the keel more even, adjust the weight around so that life would be more balanced. Right now it was atilt, listing. I toyed with my daydream, of running away to the sea. Jake had told me he was not yet ready to move in with me, and I didn't want to push him. But I wasn't sure how much longer I could keep going alone.

As the last glimmer of light faded, my courage started to come back. I thought about how I had been a wayward teenager – headstrong, unruly, a half-runaway. How I'd found myself continuing with a wayward life, just as difficult to control and predict. Like a river, I flowed with perpetual change and turbulence. But, sitting on that bench, I realised that this strange, slow adventure I was on was actually helping me find my way home. I had friends and I was strong. There was still new territory I wanted to explore. I could survive this next journey, this ambiguous, disorientating, wild way of life. I sat there for a few more moments, then got up, called Mango so he would be close to me, and walked slowly back to the boat.

It was almost as if the river rewarded me for deciding to stick with it. Gradually my boat family started to grow. Tommy and his girlfriend Becky on their boat *Phoenix* were the next to join Sam, Abbie and me in our flotilla. These two knew Sam, they had a mutual friend. Tommy and Sam liked to go for a paddle to the pub from time to time, Tommy in a kayak and Sam on his paddleboard. I loved Tommy and Becky, and we instantly all got on together as a group. There was a memorable Tommy and Becky barbecue in May on the magic bend beside Walthamstow Marshes where we were all moored. We huddled beneath gazebos Tommy and Becky had put up as we sheltered from the rain. We'd perhaps got excited about summer a bit early. Tommy, square and stoic, was at the barbecue, turning over marinated veg, which was sending steam sizzling into the air.

The heavens opened, but the rowers still rowed, and we still barbecued. Evening drew in, and the rain cleared, and the barbecue party emerged from under its tarpaulin covers, continuing into the night. I went back to my boat, in need of some peace and quiet for a moment, and watched the sun casting its golden tinge over the lush, rain-soaked grass through the window. Mango didn't want to sit still for long. He pushed his nose into my face and pawed at the front door, so we headed out, strolling a little way into a small woodland where the path split in two. I chose the sunnier fork, thin and brambly, and we followed it, making long shadows on the wet grass, to a clearing with a gnarled willow tree, and an inexplicable wooden Mad Hatter-style table with intricately carved chairs. *Where am I?* I realised I had lost my bearings. The GPS dot on my phone bounced around the virtual map, unable to find me. I was lost in London's wild again.

Mango flushed the hedges of their wildlife, emerging with sticky burrs gluing his hair together. The foliage was rain-drenched and waist high, dampening my clothes and Mango's fur. He raced ahead, alert, picking up scents, scurrying into sludgy bogs, shaking the muddied water onto me on his way out. As I walked a little further, people – young, confused, dreadlocked and wild – emerged from the bushes. I said hello, but they talked back to me in nonsense. Then, just round the bend, I spotted sniffer dogs and police taking control of an enormous sound system, and I realised they were shutting down a rave. A few more wrong turns, and then somehow I was back on the river, with huge swirling clouds above me turning orange and baby pink, like a fairytale land.

I joined Sam for a beer on his deck, which was next to mine, forming one larger, shared deck. He was wearing a crisp pressed shirt. He had just got back from a shift at the hospital. The sun was shining. The radio was playing and he had his cafetière of cold coffee wrapped in its crocheted jumper on the side. He was sitting with his on-off love who was South African and lived in New York. She was wild and smiley and had long wavy blonde hair tinted with pink, and gave me massive hugs.

"Do you fancy going down to Jam on the Butty?" Sam asked. "We were thinking of taking a wander down."

"Yeah OK," I said.

The Village Butty was a wonderful floating community hall

on a barge run by boaters Alice, Ian and James. It continuously cruised like we did, and put on workshops, events and music nights. Instead of steel, the walls were fabric which could be rolled up for events. Without an engine, it got towed by a narrowboat. Jam on the Butty was an open acoustic session they hosted.

As we approached the floating village hall, I could hear the sound of stomping feet, accordion and banjo luring us inside. On board the butty boat, dogs were swirling through the dancing crowd, rum and homemade ginger beer was being passed from hand to hand, and pots of spiced soup were being feasted on. Boat babies bounced on knees dressed in patchwork colour, faces creased with smiles, and day fell into night. It was joyously hearty. Jake joined us, his face immediately lighting me up. I adored him. He put his arms around me and lifted me into the air. I felt like I'd gone into steerage for a knees-up and was falling deeper into love like Rose on the Titanic.

My burning toes hopped across hot steel gunwales, and I knew it had all been worth it. Enduring both the weather and darkness, as well all those comments from land dwellers living behind thick walls about how it was a "mild winter" were in the past. We'd made it. It was finally summer. This, our summer, where the days were truly warm, was what we'd all been longing for, our reward. Summer brought with it more room. Dinners spilled over onto the towpath again, the roof could be sat on, and the side hatch opened. Rays of sun reflected off the water and danced across the wooden ceiling of the boat. The city also felt freshly energised. The empty parks I'd been walking Mango in for months were now swamped with picnickers. The places where I'd managed to snatch moments of quiet contemplation now filled with city land folk. The canal had become a zoo, full of tourists, dreamily muttering to each other: "Doesn't it look romantic? Maybe we should get a boat..."

Like other nomads around the world who follow a seasonal pattern of movement, Sam, Abbie and I decided to migrate. Becky and Tommy would catch us up later in the summer. We would go north out of London and into the countryside. We all longed for more nature, for bigger open spaces.

"A friend who's moored in Waltham Abbey is moving up to Cheshunt next, so we can take her spot," I said to Abbie and Sam as we shared a pot of coffee on Sam's deck in the morning sun. "It's green and lovely there, apparently, and she says there's room for three boats on the grassy patch just before the lock."

Abbie smiled. "I'm keen."

"Me too," said Sam. "Can you pass the milk?"

"Jo's coming to help me move," I said, pouring milk into Sam's coffee. "I'll find us all a good spot. Remember to find your waterways key for the electric lock. And someone told me that the second lock needs a really big shove to open as it's broken."

Jo, the girl who had made me eggy bread and had since become a good friend, came dressed in black velvet despite the heat and arrived on the same coral-coloured bike she'd had as a teen. She'd got lost and held up on the way as she always did, so we would be setting off much later than I'd planned, but she made it, as she always did. Before I knew it, I was away, heading up into unchartered territory. After more than two years of living aboard and exploring the waterways of London, I was now going further out than I'd ever been. It always surprised me how easy it was to set off. You just untied and went.

This journey was all new, all exciting. After Tottenham Lock and Stonebridge Lock and the rough grassland of Tottenham Marshes, with its wild flowers and prickly thistle growing within the abandoned damp, there was a long stretch of nothing kind of places: one of the UK's largest waste recycling facilities, an enormous sewage works which discharged treated waste into a nearby tributary of the river, a car recovery company, an agricultural recycling company which reprocessed waste from demolition sites and acres and acres of flat land with piles of crushed concrete and rough sand. In amongst the rocks stood a tiny workers' caff with a sunshine-yellow sign which read 'Lea Side Café'. This land looked film-set-like, post-apocalyptic. It was vast, and people-less. Nothing like the rest of London. There were large windowless warehouses, a reinforced concrete company, a skip hire company, a huge power station. Enormous electricity pylons followed the straight flat cut. Water reservoirs were hidden behind raised grass banks and blocked off with fences. I travelled beneath the roaring North Circular, eight lanes of cars zooming over me at seventy miles per hour, obliviously crossing the canal in a single second.

At one point, *Genesis* started to steer in a different way, her engine making a worrying sound. I put the throttle into reverse and gave it a few revs to try and shift any crap wrapped around the propeller. It didn't work. I pulled up and asked Jo to hold the boat. To undo the heavy lid to the weed hatch I had to knock the handle with a hammer. I lay on my stomach, looking over the hatch into the river. It was the first time I had done this job. Jake had done it for me a few times because he had longer limbs than me. It was like a strange sea aquarium experience. I lowered my arm into the cold water and felt around the metal shaft and prop, pulling off bits of weed. A plastic bag. I fastened the metal lid back on tight, and we carried on. There was lock after lock. At Picketts Lock, known as Alfie's Lock after the old lock keeper, a notice on the lock read: 'Every boat navigating this lock shall provide Alfie Saggs Lock Keeper with a Bounty bar placed in the box above.'

Then came lines of fully restored old working boats at South Island Marina, Ponder's End Lock, Enfield Lock and Rammey Marsh Lock. I cruised beneath the M25. *Genesis*, my home, was now in Hertfordshire. Jo cheered as she sat on the roof. We reached the fourth and final lock: Waltham Town Lock, near Waltham Abbey where I was told muntjac deer sneak around the trees, and where King Harold was buried following an arrow to the eye. It was also where the old gunpowder mills were; Thames barge *Lady of the Lea* used to transport gunpowder from here and from Woolwich Arsenal completely by sail and horse, as no engines were allowed onboard or inside the mills, to minimise risk of explosion. Four hours of captaining my small ship had passed and I was beginning to get tired.

"Jo, can you loop the rope round that bollard and hold her steady for me? I'll close the gates."

"Yep, I'm on it," she replied with a smile. Her hair was marigold orange today. Last time I saw her it'd been bubblegum blue, before that faded green, golden blonde, and deep pink.

I closed the lock gates and opened the sluices. As I stood on the bank, waiting for the chamber to fill to raise *Genesis*, I could see Jo chatting with a couple of women, and then I saw two men running towards me. They were a fair way off but I could make out mallets in their hands. I wondered why they looked so crazed. They were running with urgency, and as they got to the lock, without saying anything, they started to hammer away at the bollards that *Genesis* was tied up to. It happened in slow motion, me temporarily paralysed with tiredness.

It was then that I looked at my boat. *Genesis*, with everything I owned inside her, was tilting at a sharp angle on her side. I noticed the ropes were, for some reason, tied tightly to the bollards. Jo had got distracted chatting with the women who were interested in what we were doing and, instead of loosely looping and holding the rope, she'd knotted it. Water was gushing into the lock, raising the water level fast, while the ropes held *Genesis* tight to the side and pulled her down. I realised the men were desperately trying to chip away at the concrete bollard or beat the rope loose, to free *Genesis*, and prevent my home from flooding. I jumped onto the boat roof, knowing that if I slipped and fell in to the lock the heavy boat and gushing waters would crush and swallow me, but I was now practised at judging distances when jumping on and off boats and trusted my body's ability. I bolted inside the boat to get a kitchen knife to slice the rope, which I thought would be quicker than opening the bottom sluice gates and closing the top ones to lower the water level. All the while, my blue boat tilted more and more, the water level quickly rising. My entire home was moments from being pulled under enough to flood and very quickly sink. The men succeeded in loosening the rope before I did. With one more *chink* of the hammer, they freed it from the bollard. *Genesis* bounced back up in the water, buoyant, afloat. My heart pounded as I began realising what had very nearly happened. I'd been seconds away from losing my world.

"Thank you, thank you so much," I said to the strangers, forever in their debt.

"God, so sorry, Danie," Jo said.

"That's alright, Jo, don't worry," I said to her, and I really meant it. It was easy to make mistakes with so many distractions and so much to think about, and I valued her company far too much to make a fuss. She was younger than me and didn't have strong opinions on what we should be doing at this stage of life, or know about or want to talk about grown-up things like saving for a mortgage (I found it bleak that mortgage literally translates as 'death pledge'). She was so full of life. She released the pressure. She said yes to any invitation no matter what the adventure. She brought a spark and smile to life.

The light was just about to slip away for the night. We found a nice spot to moor just up from Waltham Abbey in Cheshunt. On either side of the river, tucked behind hedgerows, were large lakes, marshland, meadows, smaller snaking rivers, miles of winding footpaths and trails through woodland, bird-watching hides, hidden concrete gun towers and pillboxes – the remnants of World War 2 defences to protect the nearby Gunpowder Mills and ammo stores – and water-filled gravel pits. With Mango, I would soon discover it all. I pulled the boat's throttle into reverse, bringing tonnes of steel to a steady halt. Like trees that move their leaves to soak up more light, I positioned my home to face the sun to give the solar panel and me the best chance of soaking up the light we needed. Rope in hand, I jumped off the stern onto the towpath to tie up. The air's temperature was beginning to dip, and the view was perfect. The lingering light was casting everything in a glow; a photographer's dream. Jo had a gig to get to. I thanked her for her help and she cycled off to catch a train back to London.

The next morning I had to write some TV continuity scripts so went in search of a café. I found a small tearoom beside Waltham Abbey. When I went inside, the quietness was loud. It was so heavy my ears took a few moments to adjust. There was no chattering, no meetings, no noisy coffee machines, no music. I could only hear the clink of my cup as it touched its saucer, the tap of my laptop keys as I wrote. We'd made it out of the city, and I expected things to be calmer, but the peace still took me by surprise.

Once my work was done, I took Mango for a walk before lunch. We walked along a footpath crossing the small ponds, fishing lakes and shallow streams that make up the Lee Valley Park. A flash of electricity; sapphire-blue feathers flitted past me. And then a kingfisher – *zip* – skirting the hedge. All around me were flickers of bright colour, blue over by the trees, butter-yellow lilies on the lake. No one else was around. But that was it for the show – I wouldn't catch another sight of the kingfisher in amongst the leaves, thanks to Mango jumping in the water, running out and shaking wet dog all over my ankles.

It started to pour. It was the kind of rain where suddenly you're so wet it doesn't matter anymore, and you have to embrace it. The path I was walking quickly became riddled with puddles reflecting a sky storming with grey. Off in the distance, I spied a waterproofed boater I recognised, also walking a dog. It was one of my pair of boat guardian angels, Richard, the provider of the spare windlass that first day of bringing *Genesis* into London. He told me he and his girlfriend Eleni had plans to escape the grey and to move to Spain, build a couple of lovely cabins to rent out, and live in the wilderness. They were also toying with the idea of doing up another boat to give them the funds to afford to build their own dream boat. We walked together for a short while until his dog, older than Mango, got tired and turned back. Mango, full of energy, of course, carried on bounding forwards.

Later, the sky cleared and the sun reappeared. Jake came to see me, and together with dust-fogged goggles, ear protectors and angle grinder, we took it in turns to blast rust off the side of the boat, painting it with red oxide while kneeling from the canal-side. Up on the roof, my laundry was drying in the warmth thanks to Jake's newest innovation: a makeshift washing line made of salvaged wooden poles.

"If it's sunny tomorrow can we take all the rugs and blankets out onto the grass and drink coffee?" I said to Jake.

"That sounds like a great plan."

Jake handed me a big tub of strong wet-wipes and I rubbed the rust and paint off my hands and arms.

"Please can we have chickens, goats, a cat and ducks one day?" I said, standing back to survey our handiwork.

"Of course we can," he said. I threw my arms around his neck and kissed him.

A few days after I had arrived in Cheshunt, I watched Abbie and Sam slowly advancing towards me, two slow-moving gleaming boats, flat-bottomed and sturdy, as dependable as their owners. They moored bow-to-stern with me, some shuffling and pulling required to form our line before the metal mooring pins were hammered into the grass. Our heavy homes formed a small village. A feast of food, booze, tobacco and chairs immediately spilled out on the towpath, as we took in our new camp. There was no water tap for miles so we would be washing with kettles of water or in the river for the next couple of weeks. The orange of the city glowed to the south, but directly above, it was now dark enough for stars. As the night grew deeper, the flotilla grew wilder, a pack howling and singing with drunken happiness.

While Cheshunt was home, there were many communal towpath dinners. Abbie's boat *Luna* seemed to be a constant delightful source of wine, which she'd pour into glasses the moment any of us got home from work. The towpath became the dining table, and we'd eat under amazing skies on a grassy space between the towpath and the canal. With no one else around, we could really spread out. We swam whenever it was hot, when we were drunk or when we needed to wash as we were low on water. But of course, there were still practical matters that couldn't be ignored, like laundry. I spent an hour and a half cycling around with the bike trailer and Mango looking for a launderette. I kept finding dry cleaners, but no launderettes. Eventually, I found one where the owner said he'd drop the laundry to the boat for six quid, and agreed to pick up my friends' laundry if we timed it so we all needed to do a load at the same time. Getting to and from work was now by commuter train. The railway followed the river. And what had taken us four hours by boat, from Tottenham Hale to Cheshunt, only took eight minutes by train. When I got off the train after work, I'd wheel my bike through the small crowd of commuters and head in the opposite direction to them. There were no houses where I was headed.

Soon we were on the move again. I set off first, and pulled up beside a big grassy clearing with willow trees in the next place, Broxbourne, its old English name believed to mean 'badger stream'. Like Cheshunt, Broxbourne was a commuter town but I hardly visited it, spending every spare moment when not at work on the river. Here within the Lee Valley country park, surrounded by acres of green space, wild woodland, enchanting lakes and wetlands, it was easy to forget the nearby towns of Cheshunt and Broxbourne even existed. I was tucked up inside an old valley, formed by a glacial melt, where no houses stood. It was just boats and nature. I sent a message to the flotilla telling them where our new garden was. They planned to arrive the next day. Across the river in the sun, ducks snoozed on the railway sleepers that made a barrier between the river and the weir, yellow water lilies enjoyed their undisturbed edge, and dragonflies also made the most of this sunlit spot.

I hopped onto my roof to tend to my floating garden. Then, I heard a roar.

"I'll blow your bloody boat up!" I turned to see a stocky red-faced fisherman growling at me like a fat angry dog, just inches from where I was crouching to de-head flowers. My hackles shot up, my adrenaline pumped. I was ready to protect my home.

"I've fished here for fifteen years! This is my spot!"

Only moments before I had been pottering about barefoot on the roof, watering my rooftop garden and admiring my new mooring. Bees buzzed around the wild flowers and lavender, and it had felt like a mini-haven. But it was clear now that I wasn't the only person who liked this spot.

"This isn't a private mooring, or a fishing lake, or your river," I said, over his growls. "I'm allowed to moor here for fourteen days, so I'll be staying."

He wasn't listening. "It's not a proper house! I'm gonna blow it up!" he shouted, even angrier than before.

An older chap a little down the way came out to tell him off, asking him to apologise, but it riled the fisherman even more. Eventually, in a fury, he staggered away down the towpath. I dialled 999. A policeman actually came. Perhaps because we were now out of London.

"It's lovely down here," he said to me. "Never been here before, don't think I even knew it was here. I'll do an extra patrol along here the next couple of days at the end of my shift. Not a bad way to end the day."

My skin was pimpled as I stood on the stern of Abbie's boat *Luna* in a dark-blue swimming costume looking down into the river. I could hear birdsong, see a moorhen and geese swimming a little further upstream, and smell summer. I hesitated for a moment as I considered my entrance, and then with one loud splash, the sounds became different. I could feel the sting of a scrape on my behind, skin cut from catching something sharp sticking out of the boat as I'd jumped in, now open and absorbing the river water. I didn't care. The cold distracted me. Perhaps the feeling of euphoria was a tickle from billions of years before when all living things were beneath water, or a trigger of a memory of my life beginning in a womb of water. The submersion injected me with energy, rejuvenated my body, activating me like a plant

146

that was long overdue a watering. I floated on my back like an otter, drenched in happiness and soaking up the concentrated energy of this flowing river. Surrounded by the wild green of the country park, I was content and euphoric at the same time, and could feel my entire body from fingers to toes. The sounds of splashes and laughing of friends washed over me. I looked up to see Jake floating around on a paddleboard. I swam over to him and we held hands beneath the water.

After a little while I hauled myself up onto the gunwales using a tyre fender as a foot-up. River life had made me stronger, nimbler and more aware of my body's abilities, but my exit still wasn't elegant. I twisted my body round to try and place a plaster onto the bleeding gash on my left bum cheek. I'd splashed it clean, but was still worried about whether the disease-ridden river would have contaminated me.

This river had regularly bruised me. It had landed me in hospital, made me cry, but it was healing my soul. The water seemed to have some magical ability that restored me. It had required surviving, but at the same time been essential to my survival. As I watched the light bouncing off the water and projecting onto the bank, saw the dense trees which lined the river blowing in the breeze, and small ripples glistening on the river's surface, I thought: *this is bliss.*

9

It was August, my third on the boat, and my favourite month, the month that has the nostalgic feel of school summer holidays with endless days where anything can happen. Like music from youth, the sun instantly brought back feelings of wild adventure. The ripening blackberries on the canal-side hedges were deceptive – it was tempting to pick them too early, but now I knew it was worth waiting. The extra juicy, riper ones were on the other side of the river, so Sam rowed over to collect them to make a crumble for my birthday. Jake gave me ten big yellow sunflowers. And Abbie got me a book of poems from a poet who lived by the sea. All my thoughts of sinking, rusting, coming untied, being broken into had completely dissolved and disappeared into the flowing water.

A few days later, with rucksacks filled with bags of glitter, colourful clothes and small tents, most of the flotilla, along with much of the canal community, headed off to festival fields. As I wandered between teepees and patterned canvas tents filled with story-tellers, poets, musicians and performers, I encountered my extended community. We'd left our boats behind, but the soul of the river came with us. Jazzy Steve blew sax to stomping gypsy blues, Tim whirled around with a sunflower in hand, barrister Paul spun in a colourful tent amidst a cloud of bubbles, while a boater who I recognised, with her long red hair and chunky boots, served sausage and mash from her caravan and played the fiddle. I saw the guy who crashed into my boat swaying to the sound of brass with his girlfriend, while another boater friend Michelle shouted poetry about spiders on boats in a slam tent. And the ones closest to me, my boat brother Sam and boat sister Abbie, helped children walk slacklines, and bounced to Ghanaian beats in a multicoloured tent.

Afterwards, tired, soggy and covered in glitter, Sam, Abbie, Jake and I all rolled out of Sam's little car onto the towpath, laden with bags and tents. There was no more welcome a sight than our boats waiting for us in the sun at Broxbourne, nestled amongst the purple and white petals that dotted the tall grasses, and trees in every shade of green. Lazy clouds drifted above, and the slow-flowing water looked serene. Glitter shimmered and bounced off the sides of our boats.

Our water tanks were low, so, ever the addicts for sensation and now hardened to the cold, we jumped into the river for a wash. Once dried off, the four of us met back on Abbie's boat for some hammock lazing. I noticed, drowsily, that Mango's curls camouflaged him against the fake sheepskin rug on the floor. Part of the surroundings.

"Having a sort-out-my-life night tomorrow, but could cook too?" Abbie said. "You in tomorrow?"

"Count me in, Abbie." I replied

Sam looked up from the book he was flicking through. "Guess what I found emptying out the bilges just now? A little crayfish. He must've got trapped in there somehow."

"A crayfish!" Abbie said. "Cheeky little nipper."

Sam checked the weather report on his phone. "Weather's looking good tomorrow. There was going to be intermittent showers but no more, just sunshine. Good, my wooden back deck is going to get so oiled. I can't make supper tomorrow, Abbie, I'm out tomorrow night."

"I'll leave a bowl of moussaka out for you on your deck for when you get home."

"Thanks. Anyone got a set of metal files?" Sam asked.

"Yep, I do," I said. I had slowly collected a large number of tools. "Come over whenever and get them. Can anyone walk Mango for me Monday?"

"Sure, I can, no probs," Sam said.

"Thanks. I'll leave his lead on the side. Key under the usual pot."

"Does anyone need anything from B&Q, by the way, I'll be going this week at some point?" Abbie asked.

I did. "Yeah, can you get me a wire brush for the end of a drill if they have one?"

The kettle on the hob started whistling, and Abbie held a teapot in the air. "Right, enough boat chat, tea everyone?"

A comforting, content feeling flowed through me. The warm, easy feeling of belonging, of family.

Hooked on our adventure and knowing there was more to explore, we decided to do one more move north. I'd heard of a place called Roydon from another boater, and Abbie and Sam liked the idea of exploring the River Stort, so that's where we'd go. According to the spare map Becky and Tommy had given me, it would take about four and a half hours, and there'd be five locks.

I steered *Genesis* beneath a crumbling and disused old brick bridge as I set off from Broxbourne, flora growing through its cracks. Jake was with me, and I couldn't imagine life getting any better. Suddenly in front of me was a sea of small electric hire-by-the-day boats buzzing around like water bugs in every direction. I honked the horn, one extra-long blast, and slowly ploughed my way through. Fancy houses with water frontages lined the bank on my right, with smart white cruiser boats moored up at the end of their gardens. Ahead of me the river took a sharp bend to the east. Beyond the large bend was a waterside pub with a beer garden and a two-hour mooring. For years working boatmen would have stopped in these watering holes to get a beer, fill their stomachs, leave messages for other boaters, and rest their horses in the pub stables.

I steered through Carthagena Lock, Dobbs Weir Lock and Feildes Weir Lock, filling up with water and getting rid of rubbish on the way. Jake and I worked as a perfect team, chatting as we pulled ropes and opened locks as if second nature. Then, there was a fork in the river. Straight ahead, the Lea continued north onto Stanstead Abbotts, and Amwell Nature Reserve. The branch off to the right, north east, was the River Stort. A whole new river. I veered right, and suddenly everything was even greener than it had been. I was leaving Hertfordshire, and entering new uncharted territory: Essex. The tranquil, willow-tree-lined waterway twisted and flowed around glistening wet grasslands and along lines of enchanting hills. I was cruising at a speed at which scenery can be fully savoured.

In the rooftop garden box my brother built for me with scraps of wood from the towpath, wild seeds had grown into a meadow of tall yellow sunflowers, which gently swayed in the wind. Other tall stems of unknown wild flowers had bloomed too, nameless beauties, and the potted herbs had expanded. In a single swoop, the towering sunflowers all lost their heads to a low bridge, exploding into a cloud of pollen and petals. Bikes locked to the roof only narrowly missed the crushing by a centimetre or two.

I reached the village of Roydon, passed through it, and arrived at the final lock of the day, Roydon Lock. I'd heard among boaters that this lock house was home to a couple known as the 'mum and dad you wished you had'. And they were living up to their reputation. As I went through the lock, these parents of the River Stort were busy filling bellies with cake and coffee, loading boats up with bottles of gas, coal and other bits and bobs. Their smiles were as big as smiles go.

"We're always open for boaters," Steph said in her thick Essex accent, gravelled with a smoker's husk, calling to us from her lock cottage's open half-door as we cruised past. A large Alsatian jumped up on the half-door, paws over the top. "Cheese toastie? I'll bring it out to you darling... sugar in your coffee? See you later, mind me flowers! Do you fancy a nice ice cream? I've got vanilla, lemon, or toffee. Nigel, can you make some room for these people? See ya, John, you look after that leg!"

Come winter, she, her husband Nigel and their son would keep boats that navigated the waterways warm and toasty with bags of kindling and coal. Their garden was filled with walkers, cyclists, boaters, children and dogs, and outside their front door a sign read: "Welcome, Roydon Lock. Laundry service, shower & toilets, chandlery, calor gas, solid fuel." On the wooden bench by the front door lay pots of grease and mooring pins for sale, and on the wall hung a hundred-year-old cabin door. I picked up a spare windlass and a chimney hat, after mine had been blown away on a particularly blustery night last winter.

"You know, there are sometimes otters down here," Steph said, gesturing to the water. We chatted, and I immediately loved her.

Jake and I cruised on a little further upriver to where a blanket of mist had settled over an ancient meadow called Hunsdon Mead. It was bright green, but the next time we'd come here it would be painted yellow with cowslips, marsh marigolds, buttercups, giant daisies and yellow rattle. An information board said that this insect-filled grassland had been farmed the same way for six hundred years, grazed by sheep and cattle in the winter after the hay is cut in summer. It demanded to be cartwheeled in. Canada geese clattered into flight overhead in a V shape, soaring low over boggy marshes into the pink and dusky-orange sunset. Clutching the centre line, I pulled *Genesis* into the spot that'd get the most evening sun, home for two weeks.

Engine off, mooring pins hammered, stern gland twisted, starter battery isolated, brass tiller inside, kettle on. While the water slowly whistled to a boil, I messaged the flotilla who were soon to catch me up with a picture of our new home, along with details of where the secret tap was, which lock was fast to fill and the stretches that were shallow or weedy. In the morning, with Jake still asleep and no one else in sight, Mango and I ran through pockets of warm air in the green, watching the hairy, chocolate-brown cows on the other side of the river walk single file to the wetlands. In my pants and pyjama top I lay down in the meadow for a moment of sunbathing privacy.

Soon I was joined by my convoy of floating friends, and for a fortnight, we would all make the long commute from work to our latest paradise. The first back would greet the others with a bottle of something, and we drank over glassy reflections of sky on water. There, on that narrow winding ribbon of river, life was a different colour. We had died and gone to Roydon.

There were still jobs to do, of course, and I spent that first weekend at Roydon mostly hanging off the side of my boat, electrical sander in hand, a couple of feet away from the water and a hospital visit, blasting off chips of rust. In a crouched-down angled squat, thighs burning, I then painted the sides upside down. Despite the discomfort, it was gratifying.

I thought of nothing else but reaching that patch of steel and covering it in paint. I became entirely focused on small areas of metal, making sure they were properly prepped and painted to keep this floating home floating for as long as possible. Hours slipped by and my focus on the brush strokes made me forget the painful position I was holding my body in. My hands fuzzed with power-tool vibration, the muscles of my arms ached and my shoulders crunched in a multitude of clicks as I rolled them. My lungs were rust-filled. I didn't care in the slightest that my denim dungarees were covered in paint, my hair was clipped messily at the top of my head, or that I smelled of dust from sanding hot steel. I was calm, I felt right. I somehow now owned: a mouse sander, a power drill, a set of files, an angle grinder, brushes, multiple sealants, wood filler, wood stain and oil, metal paints, brass polish, goggles, a dust mask, bitumen, super industrial strength oil cleaner, extra strength glue, mounds of blue roll, oil absorbent pads, white spirit, wire cutters, a Stanley knife and wood stove paint. I shopped in DIY stores and boat chandleries more than anywhere else. It was hard to believe that I began this journey with just an adjustable spanner and a basic tool kit containing a couple of screwdrivers, a hammer and a tape measure.

Jake lifted up the decking from the front deck, cleaning underneath it and hammering nails into the pieces of wood that had come apart. He was starting to spend much more time on *Genesis* with me, cycling up to Tottenham Hale from Hackney Wick, then getting a train up to Roydon whenever he could. Nearby, Sam was also looking after his boat, sanding and restaining his back deck after it had become waterlogged. His next job was to sort his new solar panel wiring. Abbie, dressed in floating florals, was pumping out water from *Luna*'s engine bilge.

"God, hold this will you, right. Bloody boats," she grinned, laughing at the ridiculousness of what our lives now involved. She stood up to scrape her blonde waves out of her eyes into a half-bun, rolled her shoulders back and bent back down into the engine depths to suck up the remaining oily residue. "I'm going to a wedding in a minute!"

When I finished painting, I poured white spirit over the clogged brushes then onto my hands and metal-paint-splattered nails, smearing the colours and tar like bitumen up my forearms as I rubbed. The stinging smell was penetrative. I scrubbed hard, as if I were cleaning graffiti off brick, and picked out the darkness that had embedded beneath my nails. I needed to look clean enough for the Soho recording studios I would be heading to after the weekend was up.

We were free, but not footloose. Our boats required commitment. Leisure time was hard-earned. Many of the jobs needed dry weather, and so could only be done in warmer months. And no matter how many things we ticked off, something else instantly appeared. When it comes to boats, it seems Ratty was right: "You're always busy, and you never do anything in particular; and when you've done it there's always something else to do..." But, despite all the jobs, as he so wisely also told his friend Mole, "There is *nothing* - absolutely nothing - half so much worth doing as simply messing about in boats."

There was a cheeky growl in Abbie's voice as she poured glasses and stirred pots, her focus flitting from one thing to the next. Her infectious, hoarse laugh cut through noise and instantly ignited other smiles. It was Abbie's thirty-second birthday. Already drunk after a speedy pre-supper pub session in the local pub in Roydon, we'd lined our stomachs with bits of burnt banana bread excavated from the inside of a cake tin, the remains of Abbie's baking disaster earlier that day. "We prefer it burnt," we'd told her.

Amongst our flotilla crew, the ante for supper had been slowly upped, reaching its pinnacle in Roydon. Dinners had become banquets, almost wedding-feast affairs, with multiple courses and sides and tipples, everyone bringing something to add to an already hefty spread. This was to be no exception.

We had been joined in Roydon by our newest boater to the pack, Jackson, a tall, dark-eyed and impressively bright junior doctor, a year older than me, who had just bought his beautiful fifty-six-foot narrowboat, *Emmandbee*. He'd been working in a rural hospital in South Africa, right out in the savannah and surrounded by safari parks, near the Indian Ocean. He'd met Abbie and Sam through mutual friends at AfrikaBurn, a festival in the desert in South Africa based on the philosophy of sharing and community, where no money is exchanged for a whole week and you gift food and water. He had moved back to the UK a couple of months later after working abroad for four years, and rented a small third-floor flat on an old council estate in Bethnal Green, with no garden. When he came to visit us in Stonebridge, he immediately fell in love with the way of life, and bought a boat two weeks later. He came straight up to join us in Roydon. Jackson's heart pumped fast, and longed for adrenaline and dopamine, that endorphin rush of falling in love, new experiences, people, adventure.

"Come and cycle across Greece... Come to this gig... Let's have a party in the woods... Supper round mine tomorrow... Let's paddleboard up to the lake at the weekend..." he said as we chatted.

He spoke with enthusiasm. He had the ability to talk on any subject. I would discover he could learn anything new and quickly be able to teach it to someone else. That he knew the names of all the wild birds. That he could be restless, like a young hound with excess energy to burn, unable to get comfortable and settle, wanting to do everything, and often feeling as if he was missing out. Tonight he told stories of his recent visit to Sierra Leone, delivering babies by emergency caesarean section. He was planning to cruise onto the Thames, driving from the Limehouse cut – London's oldest canal, and a place once famous for the rope it produced and as a rundown slum district – to West London for an adventure, and then rejoin us.

Abbie was looking beautiful and full of life. She opened the side hatch, a window into the dark, and smoked half a roll-up, smiling and chatting to me, her rosy farmgirl cheeks becoming rounder and apple-like.

My friendship with Abbie had by now gone beyond just sharing fun times together. We practically and emotionally looked after and helped each other. We moved heavy boats, pushed open locks and bought coal together. We cycled each other's laundry to the launderette, gave each other water when we ran out, showed each other how to do and fix things even though we were no experts. We shared the phone numbers of marine engineers and electricians who work on boats, knowledge of broken water points, whispers we'd heard on the grapevine about unsafe places to moor. Abbie had become my closest river sister, my boating ally.

"Cheers!" we all chorused as we clinked glasses, standing in the small space between the kitchen and lounge. Becky, wearing high-waisted mum jeans and bright lipstick, and tucking her dip-dyed hair behind her ear, updated me on her leather-bag-making enterprise, which she ran from her floating boat workshop. She had softness and edge, was honest and savvy.

"Yeah I've left town planning completely now, going to run the bag business full time." Her hands played with the simple gold necklace that hung over her buttoned-up-to-the-top shirt.

"Amazing. Will you get a bigger workshop, or... "

"Oh Tommy, too far, you've gone too far," she cut in, overhearing a crude story Tommy was telling someone.

"Becky girl, pass me the bottle of cognac would you babe? Ooo, give that a sniff, what flavours can you taste in that?" He passed me a grapefruit-coloured cocktail. I scrunched my eyes up as I sipped it, the liquor stinging my tongue and warming my whistle at the same time.

"Yes mate, it's got some kick to it." He said, smiling.

"Lovely, Tommy," I said. It was strong and delicious.

"You're welcome, always a pleasure, always a pleasure." He passed another cocktail to Jackson.

"Cheers mate," Jackson said, before telling a story about how three kids pinched his folding bike off his front deck earlier that day. "I found them about fifty metres away in the field trying to unfold it. I was in my swimming trunks."

"What happened?" I asked.

"When they saw me they dropped the bike and legged it."

I laughed.

"So, I'll host the next dinner guys; I'm thinking Greek," Jackson announced. "Bring something Greek. Dress Greek."

Sam was chopping onions and garlic on a wooden board. "Yes mate. I'll cover myself in feta. Can we smash some plates? I'll bring ouzo."

We discussed our cruising plan and agreed on two weeks here, two weeks back in Broxbourne, then the big move back to London, staying in Stonebridge then heading back to Walthamstow and Hackney in big long cruises as the days started closing in.

The night got merrier, till our cheeks and tummies hurt from laughter. All squished up with one another, we forgot about the world. We passed dishes over our heads, bashed elbows and clashed knees, squeezed around a tiny table together. I noticed how the intimacy of the small space we occupied meant any ice was immediately broken. Our personal boundaries were torn down and there was no room for formalities. It was impossible to stand on ceremony when eating with a plastic fork, drinking wine from a mug, and sitting with one bum cheek on a fold-up chair.

After the banoffee pie was devoured, Abbie dive-bombed off the boat for a midnight swim, wearing her pants, head under, as she always did. "Time for bed?" I whispered to Jake. We walked back to my boat, which was moored next to a field under a blanket of mist. The late summer rain the day before had been heavy enough to cause the banks to overflow, and so we waded knee-deep in the river, soggy dog held above my head, to the front door.

Sam hauled up from the river twelve snappy red crayfish in his otter-friendly trap, which would be boiled and put on a plate with homemade garlic-and-lemon mayonnaise for a wild breakfast. For days we'd been feasting on these spiky pests that have invaded England's rivers, but this was our final catch of the season. It was the morning of the last day on the River Stort in Roydon heaven. Toasted crumpets and bagels, jam, marmalade and coffee were passed around the deck. Jackson jumped into the river and swam across to the marshes to run wild with the geese in sparkling bogs. It was time to leave this spot and head back into the city. We couldn't stay anywhere for long, not even paradise. The nights were drawing in, and the longer, expensive commute was beginning to tire us. The challenges of double-mooring, the risk of being broken into, a lack of privacy, and an urban garden loomed. We were headed back to where canal-side wildlife fights for survival against the growing parasitic building sites that steal sun, space and nutrients.

Just a few sloes remained for the gin foragers, and higher up in the trees, a handful of dark-purple elderberries. Summer was fading, and autumn had begun repainting the trees, smearing the green with orange, red, brown and pink, tie-dyeing the leaves from the tips. The climbing creeper woven through the hedge was bursting into red. Nature was working quietly, doing what it needed to do without making a fuss or bragging.

"I'm just going to move some things around on the roof, we've got that low bridge to get under," Jake said, shuffling the bikes, the trailer, bags of coal and kindling, enough to last half the winter, around. *Genesis* was so loaded up she looked like a coal boat, so much so that the following week a boater popped his head out of his hatch as we cruised past, asking me how much for a bag.

My usual coal supplier, who was muscular, coal-stained and bronzed, had recently stopped trading. "I'm selling up, I've got big plans," he'd shouted in thick Welsh tones over a loud pop-popping engine as he cruised past my opened side-hatch a few weeks before. He looked wild and surly on his historic pair of boats, a motor and butty strapped together. His limbs were lean but defined and his skin was weathered and sun-cooked from days outside shifting heavy bags and canisters of gas. Just by looking at him you could tell he worked hard. He was wearing clothes that looked as worn as him, fabric softened with movement and showing evidence of the day's jobs. A rolled-up cigarette lay on top of his ear beneath his shoulder-length brown waves. It was hard to guess his age; he may have looked very good for his years, or could have been much older than he actually was.

"Where are you going to go?" I shouted so as he could hear me over his working boat's noisy engine.

"Ooo, big plans. Times are changing. If you know anyone looking for a working boat and business, let them know."

He was river-bound, and reminded me of a cormorant with feathers caked in a thin layer of oil slick. Him selling up would mean coal, kindling and gas was now going to be even harder to come by.

"I'd love to be a coal lady if I was strong enough. I'll keep an ear out. See ya," I replied.

The cruise away from Roydon was calm and peaceful with only Jake, Mango and me aboard, rather than a boat full of excited people jumping around, a mere slip away from breaking a leg. Abbie would later join me in my love of quiet solo cruising, but at that time, moving for her was still novel and cause for celebration. She'd set off late afternoon, boat filled with as many people as possible, and cruise into the night, mooring up next to me with each of her crew pulling or pushing the boat in different directions. It was quite a brilliant sight. Meanwhile, Sam had always been a no-fuss boat mover, no forward planning needed, and usually chose to cruise solo, often in the dark following a long day working in the hospital.

"Cormorant," Jake said, pointing.

"Ah, missed him."

We watched to see where the bird would resurface.

I felt a sense of melancholy. Move day would usually have me euphoric, with a new exciting home ahead of me. But this time, heading back into the city, it felt different. The past few months, every cruise had taken me further away from the capital, to a more beautiful, unknown place. I wasn't looking forward to being back amongst the unsettled, unstable urbanites.

10

"Welcome to the River!" we heard Sam shout, his voice trailing off as he cycled past *Genesis*. We were back in the Lee Valley, near Broxbourne. Sam's welcome was to Jake, who had just moved most of his stuff on board and was here to stay. I'd cleared a few cupboards, and squidged up some of my books on the shelf to make room for his. After more than two years of living alone on *Genesis* with Mango, my little boat was now home for three. We both looked at each other and smiled as we heard him. A light rain was hitting the roof above.

"I love this rain. Shall we make a really nice dinner tonight? A hearty stew or something," Jake asked, sorting out his things.

"Yeah, sounds good. We need to be extra careful with water by the way, I did that big load of washing-up the other day after everyone came over."

"Cool."

I snuggled up to him on the floor of the boat surrounded by his bits and bobs. "Oh, by the way I oiled your bike chain yesterday, hopefully that'll stop it squeaking so much."

"Thanks, I thought it was sounding a bit better."

The next morning, whilst we were still rousing, Mango, who I thought was pottering about on the front deck, came bounding in with a mouthful of thick-cut ham. From outside, I could hear a male voice shouting, "You, you, I'll kill ya!"

"Oh God," I said, looking at Jake and bolting outside into

the morning sun in my pyjamas. On a boat, many conversations happen when you're in pyjamas, at least for me anyway. As I stood up outside, I could see an angry, slightly weathered elderly boater. "I'm so sorry, I'll buy you more ham!" I said. He forgave me. My now ham-less neighbour told me he had lived on his boat for over thirty years.

"I have to pick up my medicine every couple of weeks from the same place, for my heart," he told me. "It's making it harder for me to keep continuous cruising. I'm worried about what's going to happen to my river licence, you know."

"That sounds really difficult. Can you write to the Canal & River Trust, explain that at the moment you need to be close to your doctor?" We chatted for a little while. I said sorry again for Mango stealing his ham, asked him about how things had changed on the water, and wished him luck with speaking with the Trust about having a break from continuous cruising. Most of the boaters I'd met had been in their twenties and thirties, and had only been boating for a year or two. It was nice speaking with someone older. I stepped back aboard my boat to make breakfast.

Living on the boat with Jake was a breeze. He was so laid back he was barely standing sometimes. He never got angry, or stressed, or frustrated. He was always calm, and never saw anything as a problem. He seemed happy, content. But I couldn't help but wonder if he'd be happy and content anywhere. *Is he just drifting along with me?* I knew Jake could not think of anything beyond now, his mind was filled with architecture. But I could so clearly imagine little ones and a home with a garden one day.

Perhaps that was why, that autumn, when the opportunity to live on a bigger boat with a permanent mooring came up,

I grabbed it. Jake and I were at Springfield Marina in the middle of Walthamstow Marshes to pick up supplies, and I was taking advantage of the marina's tap to fill our near-empty water tank.

"I've seen that boat there for sale online," Jake said, pointing to a beautiful historic barge moored just around the bend. Its pitted, riveted steel was freshly painted a glossy dark green. It was three times the size of *Genesis*, and as we later discovered, was built in 1934 and started its life as a cargo boat carrying grain and coal on the Leeds and Liverpool Canal. Later on, in the eighties, it was driven back down to London on the motorway and converted into a liveaboard, finally coming to rest on the River Lea, near Clapton. We quickly looked up the online advert on our phones.

"I'm going to give the number a ring," I said to Jake. "Just to see if the owners are in now. It might be nice to have a look, while the water tank fills up… "

The phone rang and a man answered.

"Yes of course, come over, just give me five."

The boat was called *Ironclad*. As we walked down the few steep steps into its big kitchen, I was taken aback by the amount of space. There was a wood burner, next to which a tortoiseshell cat was warming itself, while a five-year-old boy dressed as Batman charged about on the terracotta floor tiles. Up on the curved wooden cladding hung black-and-white photographs of the boat in its working days. The owners, a couple in their early 40s, had lived aboard this boat for nine years, they told us, and before that on a narrowboat similar to *Genesis*. I fell in love with this boat instantly, and was able to imagine a future here in full colour. The more I saw, the more set my heart became. Old salvaged navy portholes and roof skylights provided light without sacrificing privacy. The young boy's room was through a half-sized Alice-in-Wonderland door, while another curved door opened onto the main bedroom, with its dark wooden walls. There was space for a full double bed. But there was more – a chunky metal door led to a workshop with a bench full of tools, and a small wooden ramp going up to a cat flap. And most amazingly of all, she came with a mooring, on my favourite stretch of the Lea, surrounded by marshland, and grazing cattle, horses. I'd be in the middle of my floating family's cruising route, so they'd never be too far away to cycle to. It would mean the end of having to move every fourteen days.

Although I'd been trying to ignore it, the waterways, like London itself, were becoming increasingly chaotic and cramped, the calm so frequently interrupted. I kept finding that stretches of river I liked had been sold off to developers who didn't consider the effect on the local environment of injecting a concentration of people into a small area. Expensive permanent moorings had been built, taking up free mooring space. It left even fewer spots for the increasing number of continuous cruisers to moor, pushing the floating community into tighter spaces. And the numbers of boaters in the city kept going up. When I bought *Genesis* there were about 770 boats without a home mooring on continuous cruiser licenses. Now, a little more than two years on, there was more than double that number. Each summer brought another wave of optimistic new boaters, but all the while no more services had been added to provide for the increase in numbers. In fact, some taps and bins had been removed. Queues at water points were longer and more common. Elsan toilet disposal points were often faulty and overflowing, and there were more bin-bags on roofs because of the lack of rubbish bins. Stretches of canal and river that were previously fairly empty because of their bad reputation were repurposed and made safe. Places I used to be able to moor easily were now more often than not chock-a-block with boats double- and triple-moored, making getting on and off with Mango difficult, and adding time to setting off. I was also finding it increasingly hard to cope with the lack of privacy that came with living next to a busy public path in central London. This boat with its private, permanent mooring could be the answer.

"Danie, it's half nine, we've got to go," Jake announced.

"Oh gosh, yes, sorry we've got to shoot off, we've both got work and need to find somewhere to moor up," I told the owners. "Thanks so much for showing us around."

We raced back to disconnect the hose before our water tank overfilled, and got on our way. We needed to find a place to moor quickly.

"We have to get that boat!" I shouted over the popping of the engine. My mind raced, swirling with energy. There were so many reasons to go for it. The stability and security of the mooring alone would be enough, but it was also big – big enough to live in for a long time. Big enough for a family.

For years I'd worked and worked, and not spent. I bought clothes from market stalls, and holidays had been budget. And so, if I could sell *Genesis* soon, with my savings and with a small loan from Jake's parents, this boat was almost in reach.

5.45am. I woke up with that sick feeling you get when your body knows it's definitely not ready to rise. With eyes half-closed, I threw a few layers over my pyjamas, and went outside to untie the ropes with Jake. The morning's cold was biting. Droplets of morning dew lay gem-like on *Genesis'* roof. With my hand on the tiller, Mango at my feet, and Jake sitting on the roof beside me pouring coffee, I slowly cruised downstream, passing a leggy grey heron, statue-like and almost two-dimensional. I admired his S-shaped neck, yellow bill and small marble eyes before he went out of sight as I steered beneath a low metal bridge. It threw us under a swathe of crisscross shadows before opening out into daylight again. The towpath's cracks were filled with plants, and the grey water bubbled with white foam. That day we needed to cruise *Genesis* for eleven hours through eleven locks, covering thirteen miles to Stanstead Abbotts. The plan was to spend the day getting *Genesis* craned and surveyed for the sale, then it would be eleven hours and eleven locks back. It was the week before Christmas so the sun would set at 4pm. There was no time to spare. As I jumped off to push open another lock next to an unnamed industrial wasteland I realised that life hadn't stopped for even a second in the past few weeks. Getting the boat ready for sale, the blur of DIY, lengthy viewings, negotiations and paperwork had finally taken its toll on me and my body couldn't do anymore. As I heaved open the gate, my fingers lost their grip on the windlass, and my body crumpled, coming to rest on the metal lock in exhaustion.

"Let me steer Danie, you go rest, I can do this," said Jake.

"Are you sure?"

"Yes, really, go in and just close your eyes for a little while, I'll call you if I need you." When Jake came to help me on move days, we'd work as a team. I tended to steer and he'd do ropes and help with locks, but we would swap as and when we felt like it. But for the first time I had no other choice than to trust Jake to steer *Genesis* without me there, completely solo, and go inside and rest for a short while. I lay on my bed and closed my eyes. My body felt heavy and sank into the bedding. The sounds inside were new and different. Usually I was at the stern next to the engine, or working the lock open. I had never been inside my boat whilst someone else took her through a lock. The sound of water gushing was loud, bumps along the lock wall sounded heavy, the windows and cupboard doors rattled. It was strange hearing all of this, but not seeing what was happening.

It wasn't long until I felt more alive, and headed back out.

"Hello you," Jake said with complete calmness. "No disasters. Do you want to take the tiller and I'll make us a cup of coffee?"

We were moving through the locks fast now in the late December chill, pulling rain-soaked ropes that made my hands raw. Pushing, cranking, pulling, jumping, climbing, steering. Hours disappeared, sliding away as we cut through water. We lost count of locks, and darkness arrived quickly. Finally, there ahead of us was Stanstead Abbotts marina. I pulled up next to prickling hedges. Mango bounced off for a wee and run around, before the three of us collapsed inside for the evening by the fire. Our bodies ached, my hands were sore and my legs were somehow scraped and bruised.

"Well done. We did it," Jake said, as we lay on the sofa in a heap under blankets.

The next day *Genesis* was high in the air, bare-bottomed and out of place, hung by a few straps to a crane that swung her across the boatyard. She was ready for Pete the surveyor to measure the thickness of the steel, and inspect every nook, cranny and inaccessible space. She did well, and was soon bobbing and floating in the water again, holding me inside, blank faced and tired. My shoulders dropped. Relief. We were closer to being able to buy *Ironclad*.

"Come and get dhal!" Abbie announced, spooning coconutty warmth into bowls and serving them from the side hatch of her boat to the rest of the flotilla, gathered around a fire that we'd built outside on the towpath in my round metal fire pit. Tommy poured spicy liquor into cinnamon-dusted glasses. "Mate, *this* will warm your cockles!" Becky dished out Christmas gifts – nature books to help us identify wildlife when foraging.

"Good book that. Good book," Tommy interjected. "Some

things are quite hard to identify, there are loads of different types which all look very similar. If I spot something I don't know now, I pick a bit and take it home to identify with this book. It takes me too long to get anywhere if I stop to identify it when I'm walking."

Sam wasn't listening. He'd started singing with his eyes closed. Claire, the soon-to-be owner of *Genesis*, was smiling and dancing at double the speed to everyone else. Lots of people had come to view *Genesis* after I posted a For Sale ad online, but Claire was a friend of Sam, and I knew would make a wonderful addition to the flotilla and take good care of *Genesis*. Abbie agreed, and so Claire, a pink-haired *pro bono* human rights lawyer who loved dancing would be the new owner. Her partner Bertie, an environmental engineer who designed low-energy buildings, sported a perfectly curled thin moustache, played the bugle and went on post-apocalyptic survival courses, would live aboard with her. I'd already done a couple of boat lessons with her, explaining the ins and outs of *Genesis* thoroughly, and written everything down in a handover pack, taught her how to steer and go through locks, filed all the paperwork of surveys and engine services into a folder, given her the contact details for boat insurance, breakdown cover and the Canal & River Trust for her licence. All that was left to do was sign the Bill of Sale.

"You just sign here, and I sign here, and that's it," I said, as we filled in the paperwork on the floor of Abbie's boat in the middle of the party.

Back outside, a man suddenly appeared from a small white fibreglass cruiser and stumbled towards the roaring firepit. His staggering came to a halt in front of us and he spluttered a belch before carrying on. In one hand he had a dirty water bottle, crumpled and over-used; in the other, a small metal cooking pot.

"Nice fire ya got gan there, vary nice. Hn. Don't spose you can lend a friend some hot water can ya, ran out of gas like, agh, ran out of gas to cook me supper. Was gonna cook pasta."

He swayed and spluttered as he spoke, wobbling dangerously close to the fire. His clothes were stained and tattered, and smelt unaired. I wondered if his boat had saved him from homelessness.

"Have a seat mate, here, let me boil you some water," Jackson said, ducking into his boat to put his kettle on.

When Jackson handed him the boiled kettle, the man stood up and thanked us in half words, scalding water spilling over his hands as he swaggered off without even flinching. Hunched, he disappeared into his dark floating den. It looked like the hole Ben and I once dug in the garden when we tried to reach the centre of the earth.

We continued with our towpath party, sitting around the fire pit in thick jackets and woolly hats, belting out songs we didn't know the words to.

Abbie came over to where I was sitting. "I'm over being single," she confessed, squeezing my hand. "I'd just love to come home, and find that someone else has made the fire."

I hugged her and poured her a large glass of red.

"You're amazing," I told her. "Someone is making their way to you right now. And he's completely, entirely wonderful, I know it."

At the end of the night Sam lit a single leftover firework to toast Jake's and my new beginnings.

"To *Ironclad,* your new boaty home!"

It was as I was packing up *Genesis* that I saw him. The contents of cupboards were shoved into bags, then bags into bags, then bags back into cupboards because there was nowhere else to put them. Then, out of the window, I spotted someone I recognised – the little blue-eyed boy who, as a baby, ate the flowers my very first night on the water. Much bigger now, sitting confidently on the roof of a passing boat. He'd grown. So had I.

The long to-do list in my mind felt heavy and wearisome. I washed coal dust from small corners. I filled the engine room cupboards with new ropes, fenders, paints, and a windlass. Finally, Jake and I emptied out *Genesis'* insides. And then, in the biting cold of January, we carried everything we owned over into *Ironclad*.

I hadn't had much time to prepare for this departure, my abandoning of *Genesis*. As it had always been before, there was no time to dwell, to reflect, and I hadn't had a moment to sit and readjust to the unknown ahead. Now, moving onto this barge with Jake, with a mooring in a marina with all the facilities I could need, life was going to be very different. I was sure that being part of a new, less fluid boating community within the marina would be wonderful. Boat children played on a wooded island, a heron fished by my new neighbour's boat, and the sky here was vast. My favourite area to walk in London, Walthamstow Marshes, was tucked right behind these boats. I knew I would enjoy the stillness. But I wondered whether this mooring would mean missing out on impromptu towpath parties. Would I be invited to suppers aboard my new neighbours' boats? Would I continue to be part of this tight network of continuous cruisers, a community like no other, who refuse to let money cross hands and only make payments in favours or booze? Would I still see Abbie, Sam and my flotilla now they were no longer next door? I tried to think only of the positive things. A new year was about to begin. I had a home. A home with Jake. I could finally begin to settle.

Except that's not exactly what happened.

11

There wasn't much untangling to do. Jake had even fewer belongings than I did, and although our friendship groups crossed, our lives hadn't become so intertwined that one would be left empty.

At first I had been preoccupied by the wonderful novelty of a permanent mooring. For the first time in two-and-a-half years I had a washing machine, unlimited access to water and a fridge. There was a tap right beside the boat so when the water tank was low, instead of having to cruise my boat an hour or two to a tap to fill up, I could just pop outside and connect the hose and fill the tank. There was no longer any need to be super sparing with water; I could now wash myself daily. In winter, we still had to keep a fire going day and night, but I could also have an additional electric heater in the bedroom and not have to bear the chill on my skin every time I got changed. Bedsheets didn't feel damp with cold. I still didn't have a postcode though. This wasn't a residential mooring, it couldn't be used as an address, the postman did not come here, and I could not use the marina to register to be on the electoral roll. To own a boat at the marina you had to be registered as living at a different address, and the mooring agreement stipulated berth holders couldn't stay aboard their boat full time. Neighbours split their time between houses and boats, and Jake and I had to spend some nights sleeping elsewhere each month. And like before, there was still much to do, a toilet to empty, steel to be maintained, an engine to look after, a to-do list to get on with. Jake and I fixed things, sanded, painted, installed new solar panels, batteries and an inverter, sealed windows, cemented the stove, polished bronze windows, made use of the electricity to run power tools.

Sometimes it felt like cheating. One night, a thunder storm rumbled in and lit up the windows with flashes. The winds were whipping heavily, and rain hammered hard onto the roof, throwing down punches of heavy wet in waves. I thought of how *Genesis* would have been getting pulled about, fenders and ropes squeezing and groaning. But here, in the shelter of the marina, and on a wider, heavier boat, home stayed steady. An SOS WhatsApp came through on my phone from Jackson. His ropes had snapped and *Emmandbee* was now loose and drifting. Another message. This time a friend's electrics had gone and he was desperately trying to bail out water he had discovered beneath the floorboards of his boat. Becky and Tommy were also wrestling with the winds. Their wooden canoe had flown off the roof of *Phoenix*. *Ironclad* held her ground and stayed attached. It felt weird not being with the flotilla on nights like this.

We had gone from living in places no one went at night to having a boat somewhere surrounded by a tall metal fence with 24-hour CCTV security. I felt safe for the first time and stopped jumping when Mango barked. I didn't worry about strangers breaking into my boat. People couldn't stare through my window anymore. I also began having some routine. For the first time in years my journey to work stayed the same each day. Cross the bridge over the Lea, wave hello to the café owner, cycle north along the potted towpath past the cranes with the cormorants drying their wings, bump into a boater, cross though Markfield Park, up and down the hill to Seven Sisters and jump on the Victoria line. Each day Mango and I walked through Walthamstow Marshes, which were hidden behind the marina. I saw a place change through each season rather than just a two-week snapshot. But with the security and permanence came rules. We couldn't just have a firepit next to the boat, Mango wasn't allowed off the lead until we were out of the marina gates, we were only allowed to use marina-approved engineers rather than the people I had come to trust. The security also came with the expense of pricey monthly mooring fees.

Sounds became familiar on this new boat, rather than changing every two weeks. In bed at night, with moonlight breaking through clouds above our heads, sometimes we would hear a helicopter chopping the sky. Sometimes the sounds of a large Jewish celebration would drift down from Stamford Hill. But mostly, it was completely and utterly silent. No one was allowed to double-moor us, so there were no noisy feet stepping over and rocking the boat. We were on the non-towpath side of the river so there were no snippets of strange conversations from the stream of passers-by or drinkers trying to keep warm on benches beside the boat. I no longer needed to holler to the coal boat man for new bottles of gas if I ever saw him driving by, I could buy them from the marina at a time that I was free. I bought food from the same shop. I thought it would feel like home, and in a lot of ways it did: the community was wonderful and welcoming, the marshes and the Lea felt like where we were meant to be. But in some ways it didn't feel completely like home. The annual mooring agreement was at the mercy of a marina manager who I found intimidating, unfriendly and entirely unpredictable. The mooring conditions and monthly fees could change anytime.

Eventually, the long winter gave way, and blossom and bluebells grew. I breathed in the smell of creamy sweet elderflower on my walks, the wet ditches filled in with tall cow parsley, the hedgerows woven through with pink dog rose. We had made it to spring. Jake and I made new friends with our marina boat neighbours. We were in a cul-de-sac of seven boats and there were suppers and cups of tea and regular chit chats. We all took it in turns to walk our dogs. We welcomed two newborn boat babies into the community, and sang songs for them on the island. We watched boats being craned in and out of the marina to get their bottoms blacked to prevent rusting. With each craning, the boats were held high in the air upon blocks of wooden railway sleepers, like steel tree-houses. In the morning their owners would climb down ladders from their front door to go to work. When the boat with a mooring directly behind *Ironclad* went up for sale, Sam bought it so he could get the mooring. He swapped that boat for his boat and put *Madame George* there, our boats becoming next-door neighbours once more.

When summer arrived in June, after six months of staying still, Jake and I took *Ironclad* out of the marina and onto the river for ten weeks to join the flotilla for the annual migration. At seventy-two feet long, fourteen feet wide, over eighty years old, *Ironclad* was a sight to behold. People stopped and stared and waved and told us how wonderful she was, how nice it was to see her out on the water. My brother Ben came for our first voyage on her. It was a whole new adventure. Tommy and Becky on *Phoenix* travelled directly behind us, ready to help if anything went wrong on our first leg. *Ironclad* steered well and I quickly understood her. She had slow but heavy momentum, required more warning before stopping, and had to stay more to the centre of the canal because she was deeper. I needed to honk the horn more often so other boats knew to make room for her, and I had to concentrate harder when steering through narrow bridges. I could do that. But putting her into reverse to slow or stop her took some welly and might. It took more strength than I had, so at the locks I had to hand over the reins to Jake and take up rope duty, pulling the magnificent beast in with enormous thick ropes and then pushing her off again.

That summer was as glorious as the one before. We stopped in Stonebridge first, then Cheshunt, Broxbourne and Stanstead Abbotts, cruising with Abbie, Sam, Jackson, Tommy, Becky, Alice, Ben, Claire and Bertie, our boats forming a small village each time we moored up. We moved either at the same time or within a couple of days of each other, mooring bow to stern, creating an organic river house-share, a kind of family with separate private spaces but a shared garden of front decks and towpath. We knew where each set of spare keys were, whose plants needed watering, which switches had been left on by mistake and what pins to hammer in harder during strong winds. Suppers were often communal, and doors were often left open. For ten weeks we paddleboarded, kayaked, ate round fire pits, barbecued at sunset, jumped off our boats into the river and swam over and over, ate breakfasts together, discovered more lakes and paths, drank Tommy's cocktails, smoked roll-ups, danced into the night. For my birthday the flotilla made me a treasure hunt, with clues hidden on boats, in crayfish pots, within towpath bushes, all handwritten on tiny scraps of paper. And then, in August, after just eight months aboard *Ironclad* together, Jake and I broke up.

Looking back, there was one conversation that stuck out.

Jake had spent the day on the towpath doing something with concrete and bamboo.

"It's pretty hard mixing concrete without a cement mixer," he said, coming back into the boat for a cup of tea.

"What are you making, again?" I asked.

"I'm trying to build a model of the water tower I'm designing. I need to start on some more drawings tomorrow. Oh, I taught Mango 'bang!' today. Look." Jake got up off the sofa, making Mango instantly excited. "Mango, Mangooo, ready, ch ch bang! ch ch bang!" Mango did a very fast spin and high five. "Oh, well, he was meant to play dead, he was doing it earlier outside."

"Maybe there's just not enough room on the floor there."

"He seems to be more sleepy after playing games than running about through the park for an hour," Jake said, sitting back down on the sofa.

"Really? Hm, OK, I'll do more tricks and games with him. One day I will manage to tire him out."

I was putting off asking the question I wanted to ask, killing time with an ordinary conversation, not knowing how to say what I wanted to say. We'd now been together three years, living forever in the present, almost like teenagers. This was to be the first mention of a future. I had to know. I took a breath.

"Have you ever thought about children, whether a family is something you'd want one day?" I asked, terrified of what he might answer.

He paused. A painful silence that showed no sign of being broken. The length of nothingness was unsettling, I could almost feel my womb hurting.

Then Jake said, "I can't quite imagine it. I've never thought about children at all before... It's just something that's so far off thinking about for me."

Things weren't quite the same after that. We tried to carry on as we had before. I tried to go back to loving him the way I had before that pause. But the rabbit-in-the-headlights look of fear in his eyes wouldn't leave me. *Perhaps he'd become sure*

in time, change his mind, as we got on with life in our barge. I could just give him more time to be sure, I thought. *Don't give up on someone who loves you.* He was two years younger than me, still studying to be an architect and I was his first love – I understood that he was unsure and unable to think about having a family. Perhaps in time he would. But my unconscious intuition told me I could no longer hold on to his maybe. Jake could not think ahead yet in the way that I could. He was at the very start of his career, and that was his focus. After seven years of doing voice-overs, and approaching thirty, my priorities were now the other way around. Our lives weren't in line. I needed my future to be clearer, more certain. I had to listen to what it wanted. I had to force myself to move on, even though in losing him, I was also losing everything I hoped and longed for. I wasn't just losing him, I was losing dreams of love, of settled life, of safety. I was losing the family I hoped I'd have in the near future.

We were moored in Hertfordshire when I told him I wanted to end it – in the middle of Amwell Nature Reserve, a glistening wetland filled with birds, dragonflies and damselflies near a place called St Margarets. All around us were lakes, grasslands and wildlife. I have no memory of the actual words I said to him, but I remember helping him pack up his books and clothes, in a practical way, as if what was happening wasn't really happening. His clothes disappeared from the rail in the cupboard, and the gap on the shelf where his books had been stared at me.

The day he moved out I cycled down the towpath to a patch of grass, threw my bike down, looped Mango's lead onto my ankle so he wouldn't leave me, and collapsed on my back. I sobbed up into the sky. I sobbed until the sobbing slowly stopped, and I was just quiet lying on the grass.

The first week after Jake left felt strangely calm. There was a sense of relief that a decision had been made. Jackson took Mango and me for a slow and peaceful paddle on his paddleboard two miles up the Lea to Ware and back. In my blue swimming costume, I sat towards the front end of the paddleboard, bare legs folded, with Mango standing in front of me. Jackson stood upright behind us and paddled. In silence except for a few words about coots and ducks, the three of us glided upriver, enjoying the quiet. I loved being on the paddleboard. It was soothing seeing the water from that perspective, without the sound of a boat engine. It was meditative, and settled my mind after what had just happened. After a mile or so we spotted a lake through the trees on the bank and decided to jump off for a quick dip. The large lake, once a gravel pit, was surrounded by pockets of woodland. It felt undiscovered. We glimpsed the neon green and blue of dainty red-eyed damselflies zipping above the pondweed, hunting for midges and mosquitoes. We got in and swam.

Over the summer Jake and I had mastered the teamwork required to steer *Ironclad*. Jake knew I couldn't get her home without him and came back a week after we parted to help me bring her back to the marina. We cruised for two long days, driving *Ironclad* for seventeen hours in total, taking her through fourteen locks. There wasn't much time for talking. The journey took strength, concentration and stamina. We slept in separate rooms but I was too exhausted to think about how strange it all was. When we finally arrived back at the marina, and pulled *Ironclad* into her mooring spot, bodies aching, Jake helped me tie ropes. Then we said goodbye for the last time. And there I was. On a big, big boat, alone, with my dog, surrounded by marshes in London.

I thought about selling up, but I wasn't ready for more change. I had made friends with my neighbours, I had begun making this boat my own, I couldn't bear the thought of learning another boat. I withdrew my savings once more and bought Jake's share of *Ironclad*. I became entirely responsible for about forty odd tonnes of riveted steel, a vast barge with windows salvaged from a warship and an engine from an Albion lorry. She was an incredible ship, but once Jake and his things had gone, and it was just me and Mango left inside, she felt so unbelievably enormous. When I spoke, my voice even sounded different in the emptied space.

There was a lot I needed to learn. Jake knew which bolt on which pipe to twist near the boiler to get the bubble out when you accidentally let the water tank run empty during a bath. I spent three hours on the kitchen floor with a spanner trying every nut and bolt, running taps, turning the water pump on and off, all the while Mango sitting close by and intently watching as he always would when I did something, as if to help me, until I worked it out. Jake had met me on the bridge over the river to the marina to help me carry bags of food shopping. I started borrowing the neighbours' wheelbarrow to carry the load. Jake used to help walk and feed Mango. I went back to doing all the walks, and neighbours helped me out if ever I couldn't get back in time. I got around it all – my years of living on *Genesis* alone had shown me what I was capable of: I just needed to use all of what I had learned again.

I was busy. On purpose. The more DIY I did, the more things I thought needed doing. I carpeted a room, got in decorators, sealed windows, sanded and painted a lot of steel inside and out, touched up scratches with bitumen, sanded and painted cupboard doors, painted the stove, painted mirror frames, sanded kitchen surfaces and tables and oiled them, bought new brass lights, got the wooden floor sanded and varnished, got new kitchen tiles, got the engine serviced and parts reconditioned. The list goes on. I walked the marshes of Walthamstow morning and night. I wrote, I did more TV voice-overs, I formed new floating friends in the marina. I cycled to see the flotilla for suppers. I tried to not miss Jake. But whenever I washed, I missed him. It was the only time I couldn't busy myself with things that needed doing. I would realise as I washed my hair that I missed the way he did things, the way we were. I missed silly things I hadn't paid much attention to before: his unbelievable calmness in situations that others would find stressful, how we would just chat and chat. I missed his friends, and his family, his wonderful parents who'd welcomed me into their beautiful home. From time to time, Mango and I would go with Jake to visit his parents in the old thatched cottage he grew up in, out in the Buckinghamshire countryside. Flowers of every colour filled the garden, which led to a bluebell wood and fields. Through the teal-green front door, there were wonky ceilings, oak beams, and red bricks around the fireplace. I cried once, while soaking in the pale-blue bathroom with its wobbly walls and uneven floor, overwhelmed with how calm it was, how amazing his parents were. Now I mourned the loss of the life I'd dreamed I'd have with him.

Autumn came, and each morning I would wake to the sound of a flock of noisy Canada geese getting closer, louder, and louder. Dragons. They were my wakeup call throughout autumn and winter in this urban valley. I would turn my head on the pillow to look upwards, and through the roof light above my bed a huge flock flew over exactly on time. The honking came to a crescendo. The last birds in the V flew past, and the screeching petered out into the distance. In the evening, they would fly back the other way. An orange glow would fill the sky, and the flocks of geese would appear overhead in Vs. They took it in turns to lead, the hardest position, before falling back into line and taking advantage of another bird's slipstream. I remember sitting there on the deck watching a sunset turn to pink and baby blue. As I sat taking in the sky, I wondered where the geese might be going, and how they knew which way to fly.

Soon, my fourth winter aboard came around, the grass turning crunchy with ice crystals, mist rolling over the water in the early mornings. The magic bend looked more beautiful than ever. I walked and walked through the marshes, hosted the flotilla Christmas party, walked the neighbours' new puppy. I longed for spring once more.

Now that I had more time to myself I started reading. I mostly read true stories; I liked hearing about people's lives, their different worlds. Suddenly the idea came to me that I would write this story. It was like buying the boat. Once I decided on writing, I went at it with full momentum. I wrote aboard amidst all the ridiculous boat distractions, in twenty-three packed and noisy London cafés, two bookshops and one library. I wrote in two small Airbnbs, both by water, in rural Devon for seven weeks alone, and barely saw anyone. I became so immersed it was sometimes difficult to get my head out of book world. It was these months and months of reflecting and writing that helped me truly understand what had happened when I was fourteen, something I hadn't really properly comprehended until the words were there on a page looking back at me. It was this that gave me the courage to do something I never thought I would.

Sitting on the top step of *Ironclad* by the hatch one day, looking out on to the water, a rush of bravery surged through me. It came out of nowhere and took me by surprise. It was an impulse that was impossible to ignore, and demanded to be acted upon quickly before it disappeared. I was shaking as my hands tried to place and roll tobacco into paper.

I lit it, and picked up my phone.

101

"Can you tell me what's happened?" a voice said down the phone, quicker than I was ready for. I inhaled my badly rolled cigarette, and went to tell this stranger my secret from all those years ago. But then, in a single second, the rush of confidence vanished, and I hung up. As I sat silent and motionless on the top step with wet eyes looking out onto the River Lea, I wondered, *would the police even believe me?* As with around 90% of those who are raped, I knew my perpetrator. Afterwards, instead of running away and calling the police, I lay next to him, clothes unripped. *Maybe this is all best just left in the past. I've shared my secret, I told Jake, I've written it down, maybe that's enough.*

But what if he's still hurting girls?

I wanted to speak to Jake, but I knew I couldn't. Then, the police rang me back. *I have to go through with this, however hard it is.*

I attempted once again to summarise my most private and life-changing experiences with a stranger on the phone. Soon, two male policemen, who admitted they were not trained in this kind of crime, were sitting in my boat and writing my statement nonetheless. I sat there alone with these two men, what happened to me becoming an incident scribbled down on a stranger's notepad, me becoming a victim, damaged.

Weeks of no news followed. Eventually I was called in to my local police station in Stoke Newington to make a video statement. I was told two specialist officers would meet me outside. I stood waiting there for forty minutes. With each minute of waiting, my bravery diminished. With each minute I got closer and closer to not going through with it, going home, to never speaking of it again. I worried about seeing someone I knew on the street as I waited. What would I tell them I was doing? Then, the officers arrived. We went inside.

"In this room there are cameras in all the corners so we'll be videoing everything you say." A female police officer said. "I need you to tell me everything, in as much detail as you can. Even the smallest of details, however insignificant you think it may be, could be really important for us in our investigation."

"OK. I'll tell you everything I can remember, exactly how I remember it."

Painful memories that had finally stopped haunting me were refreshed, more vivid than I'd ever allowed them to be before. The unwashed testosterone smell of his pale teenage skin seeped into my mind. I was reminded of the feel of his seventeen-year-old body, broad and lean, which somehow had unrestricted access to me. And now the memory had been re-mastered in full colour, the taste of his chest refreshed in my mouth. I could see him behind me after reading him my letter to ask for it to stop. Me hopeless, complying and removed from my own body to minimise the trauma of him taking me again. Him not pulling out, seemingly unfazed by any risk of pregnancy. The dread of going through the embarrassment of asking a chemist for a morning-after pill. Lying there for a while after he'd finished, another piece of me taken. Me longing for love and enjoying his cuddles, him knowing this would make me come back, believing I was cared for. Him taking me home on the back of his moped, a spare helmet just for me.

Telling the police felt like opening up the wounds that the river had healed and then pouring white spirit in them. He was arrested a couple of days after I gave my statement, questioned and released on bail while the police investigated. But I had no idea what was going to happen next. An emotionally draining three months of no news followed. I wasn't allowed to be told anything. After speaking with the police I did some Googling. I read that rape is not only a massively under-reported crime in the UK, but also only 5.7% of reported rape cases end in a conviction. I started to wonder whether it had been worth putting myself through it.

I sat in a strange, nondescript room, with nondescript furniture. It was the only empty room available that we could talk in. In front of me was the investigating policewoman who'd called me into Stoke Newington police station. Her expression was featureless, a gentle smile impossible to read. This stranger who liked hard evidence and working with exact times and dates – all of which I had none of to report – had the power.

"A senior officer has now reviewed the case," she said. "Unfortunately, he doesn't feel there's enough evidence for a conviction. We don't want to put you through a court case if there's not a strong chance of him being convicted. It means we won't be investigating any further." I sat silent. She paused. "Your statement and video account will remain on his record, and should any more information come to light it will be reopened."

Her words drifted through the air of this strange room like those clouds of fluffy tree seeds that hover above the water in spring, taking their time to settle. My eyes flickered, my lips opened a little and then closed. I'm not sure if I breathed. After a moment that lasted for I'm not sure how long, I asked what had happened to the other girl, the girl younger than me who had told me that he had raped her. The policewoman said she couldn't tell me much, except that he hadn't been convicted, that they'd found the girl's video tape from all those years ago and watched it back, but since she'd talked about what had happened to her, not me, it couldn't be used as evidence in my "case".

"Don't think this means we don't believe you." She said.

"We do."

I walked out of the police station, and stood amidst the racket of Hackney's streets.

Then I went back to the river.

Daylight slowly drifted into the boat through the portholes and skylights as I made a pot of coffee, brightening the rooms with gold minute by minute. Mango was eager to adventure, and sat on the top step by the door, eyes wide asking me if we could go now. "OK," I told him, and put my wellies on. Outside, Mango could smell the waterfowl sleeping in the boggy ditches.

"This way," I said, keeping him distracted. A heron was perched on the old disused iron bridge and swans nested below. I knew they'd be there. "Leave, Mango." He had sniffed a little too close to them. We came to the fork in the path where he'd wait for me to let him know which way we were going. Left led to the low bridge and the magic willow tree. But today, we were going to turn right. We passed through the kissing gate to winding pathways lined with watery plants and into a woody wonderland. I was truly out-of-the-way but still in the city, enclosed by branches of pollen-filled trees. Mango was in smell heaven and somehow already mud-caked. He looked at me to say thanks. We walked through the arches of trees and emerged into the sky-wide meadow. Overhead, a bird of prey, perhaps a buzzard or a kestrel, hovered and flirted with the sky, scouring the grassland for a vole breakfast. In the waterlogged land, the ground was boggy, and my feet sank into the sodden soil, blades of droplet-covered long grass dampening the patch of legs above my wellies and all of Mango's curls. Large puddles decided my route, not a map. The grazing cattle watched me go towards the boardwalk. It was the perfect wooden wedding aisle and led me back to the mist-covered river where water flowed south towards the Thames at Limehouse and then out into the sea.

I treasured these small walks, these wanderings where I didn't need to think, or bring anything with me. Walks where if it rained and I got wet, it didn't really matter. I could just go on, knowing home was around the corner and I couldn't get too lost if I stayed reasonably close to the water's edge.

I didn't know it back then, but I'd been making a pilgrimage. But instead of one long epic trek, mine had been broken up into a series of morning and evening walks, and of over a hundred slow boat journeys. The more time I'd spent on these waterways, the more he, that summer, disappeared. These watery wanderings had cleared my mind and re-made me.

Towards the end of this fifth spring, the flotilla were back on the magic bend once more. We barbecued into the nights whilst wrapped in scarves and blankets, excited too early for summer again. When summer came around, and the wildflower seeds I had sown in my planters began to bloom, talk of the annual migration out of the city began. I knew I couldn't cruise this big ex-working boat alone, and so I decided to leave *Ironclad* where she was and get the train and cycle up to join everyone for evening suppers and weekend swims, sleeping over on Jackson's sofa on *Emmandbee*. In August, the flotilla came back to London and were back at the magic bend. In the marina, hundreds of golden orange and yellow petals lined the wall. Sunflowers, my favourite flowers, reaching towards the sun.

But things were about to change once more. The flotilla was transforming into something new, my close floating friends heading off for new adventures. The people around me were beginning to settle. My brother Ben had got a job as a DT teacher. He was now teaching children to make things in a big workshop filled with every tool and material you could imagine.

He had got engaged and was moving into a little brick cottage. Mum had fallen in love with the cook at the care home where she worked. He made her laugh and smile, and cooked her delicious meals. They'd moved into a small rented flat together. One of the first things Mum did after they moved was to make the garden nice, and paint colourful patterns all over the shed. Dad had finally found true love. His Scottish girlfriend helped him clear his flat, and after multiple skip loads he put it on the market and moved into her house in the country. They'd go on long walks together, listen to live music in old pubs and cook up tasty suppers. He said I could come visit, that Mango could come too. I'd heard Jake was back on the water, that he'd bought a boat of his own and was continuously cruising. He had fallen in love again, become qualified as an architect and still loved walking and camping in the rain.

I decided I couldn't manage *Ironclad* on my own any more. My mind toyed with options, and I scribbled down ideas. A cabin, a campervan. But none of these felt right. I needed to be attached, to belong to one place. I needed bricks and stones and foundations, a home that wasn't going anywhere, that couldn't rust, sink, or get battered in wind and rain. I put *Ironclad* on the market.

But then the unexpected happened. Just when I thought I needed to reconcile myself to being completely self-sufficient, romance blossomed with a boater. I had known Ed for a few years. We'd first met on the water. Our boats were double-moored and we chatted across our front decks. Mango was a puppy then, and inspired Ed to get a boat dog of his own – a Spaniel-Yorkshire-Terrier-Poodle mix he called Manouche (French for gypsy), or Manny for short. Manny was black and brown and had little dots for grumpy eyebrows. Ed was smiley and warm. He had curly brown hair and blue eyes, wore jazzy shirts and often had a head torch round his neck. He worked as a lighting designer, could sing, play instruments and speak different languages. He had been on the water the same amount of time I had, continuously cruising, and had also moved a lot growing up, being born in Singapore, living in Canada and then Switzerland where his parents settled. He lived aboard his seventy-foot long, leaf-green converted historic working boat where, a couple of times, he'd hosted my flotilla for a cheesy raclette supper. Over the years we had sporadically found ourselves moored nearby for a week or two and ate together with boat friends, but we were always heading in the opposite direction, him usually heading west, me usually heading east.

On my thirtieth birthday, after a fairy-lit party with my floating family on the grass by the River Lea, we kissed. Two weeks later, camping in Devon and falling in love, he asked me to live with him on his boat. It was a daunting decision to recommit to the water. After more than four years of being a water nomad I had made the decision to leave and I was one week away from handing over the keys to *Ironclad* to her new owners. I'd booked a small Airbnb in a field by a river in Devon for one month with the hope of finding a home by the sea. That's as far as my plan had got.

"I can't survive the city for much longer, I can't keep on moving," I told him.

Ed hugged me. "Let's travel on the water together for one more year. Make my boat your home for now, and in the meantime, we can search for our perfect house by the sea."

And so I did.

EPILOGUE

It is Autumn, 2017. The flotilla is moored up on the banks of the Lea by the marshes of Hackney, but it has changed form. Abbie's boat *Luna* isn't in sight. She and the kind and caring man she has fallen for, a Spanish teacher, are moored a little downriver and are busy planning their new shared life in Guatemala, where they'll live next to the sea. Abbie's going to work in a clinic, and her partner will teach local children. I cried when she told me she was leaving, but was so immensely happy for her. She said even though she's leaving the water, she will always keep it close by. I said I would too.

Sam's boat *Madame George* is also missing from the fleet. He decided to follow his dream of working out in South Africa as an HIV researcher. He quit his job in London, left his boat in the care of his sister, and went to South Africa without a job lined up. It was a gamble, and it paid off. He managed to get the work he wanted at the University of Cape Town. He didn't just move for work. "I just need more outdoors, more nature," he told me before he left. When we last spoke, he said he could see Table Mountain and the ocean from his window. It made me smile. Before he arrived in South Africa, he also achieved his biggest goal yet. He went to Yosemite National Park in California and climbed El Capitan, almost 1,000 metres of vertical sheer granite rock, in a single day. He told me it was one of the most beautiful and profound experiences of his life.

I can see *Phoenix* though, still with the flotilla. Tommy and Becky have just bought a ramshackle old barn by the sea in Devon with an apple orchard and space for growing lots of food. They plan to move there once they've fixed up the roof and heating, and get married in the garden. Their baby is almost due. Her birth certificate will list "*Phoenix*, River Lea, London" as the Place of Birth.

Next door is *Emmandbee*. Jackson has started his specialist training in endocrinology and is getting all geared towards another six-month placement in Uganda trying to understand more about diabetes and high-risk pregnancy. He has fallen in love with a beautiful girl who sings and plays strange instruments. They met whilst cycling in the Lea Valley. They got caught in the rain and drank pints in Broxbourne. She has a campervan and is now thinking of becoming a boater and joining us.

There is *Genevieve*, home to Alice and her love, Ben. They love boat life, exploring parts of London they never normally would, being outdoors, having friends pop in unannounced, making different commutes to work every couple of weeks, taking in the different seasons and weather. Alice told me how she and Ben love lying in bed and looking out of the window at the different views, the different bird-lives, people, buildings, listening to the snatched bits of conversations you hear when people walk past. Living aboard has allowed Ben to set up his own business making furniture. They've been talking about one day moving *Genevieve* closer to Bristol or Bath.

And, another boat, dear *Genesis*, home to Claire and Bertie. After two years aboard, they are still enjoying being able to escape London whilst still living in it, discovering parts of the city they never knew existed, being packed in like sardines at dinners on boats. They have stayed together with the flotilla, the family. They wonder if they will ever want to move off the water. They told me living aboard *Genesis* gives them a sense of independence and resilience that they didn't have on land, and that when the zombie apocalypse comes they're planning to escape to Roydon.

Right in the middle of the flotilla is *Cambourne*, Ed's long ex-coal boat. I can hear the sound of music drifting out and I know the whistling kettle is warming up on the hob. Mango is bimbling about by my feet, all rain-curled. The Lea's slight foam is marking the verge, and I'm standing on the towpath, the border between land and water, with my boxed-up belongings. I'm thinking about what was, and what is about to be. I'm wondering if any bit of this River Lea in front of me will make it to the sea. The water is kicking off cool air, and the day's rays are shining and reflecting in its wet. I'm content, and feel like I did when I was ten, lazing on the warmth of the shed roof with Ted the cat, soaking up the sun and daydreaming into the sky above. I'm about to enter my fifth winter, my fifth year aboard and my tenth year in London. I'm about to take another leap of faith in love and in these city waters. I am, once more, standing in that space between the previous and the new unknown, the brilliant and enchanting threshold of one thing ending and another beginning. I'm a nomad, and I'm dreaming of settling. But this time I'm closer to finding the land I will plant my roots in. Home is just around the next river bend.

ACKNOWLEDGEMENTS

Although the words in *Afloat* are my own, many people worked hard to help this book make its way to you. I want to say a huge thank you to:

My literary agent and friend, the wonderful Rebecca Carter, for your immediate faith in my book, support and guidance through the world of publishing which I knew nothing about, and for all the late nights of meticulous editorial work which pushed me to write better. You went above and beyond and I'm forever grateful. And to the fantastic team at Janklow and Nesbit UK.

My editor Susannah Otter for being brave and investing in my book, for your passion and enthusiasm. Thank you to your clever colleagues at Quadrille and Hardie Grant for their hard work in designing, producing and raising awareness of *Afloat*.

The talented Eleanor Taylor for the brilliant illustrations inside the book and for such a beautiful cover. And Maisie Noble for illustrating the map of my world which I love so much.

My friends who read parts of, or whole drafts of early versions of the manuscript along the way. Your thoughtful and constructive comments, careful edits and encouragement were invaluable and hugely appreciated; Eleanor Winter, Charlotte Tottenham,

Jack Milln, Laurie Watkins and Michelle Madsen.

Natalie Holiday and James Thake at Wise Buddah for making my voice-over diary work around the large amount of time I needed to write the book. Without your hard work I wouldn't have been able to afford the time to write this, or afford a floating home in the first place.

Laura Payne and Jack Rowley for your help making a lovely video trailer for my book.

Over the near six years of living on the water, I met and enjoyed the company of many wonderful, kind people who kept me afloat in many different ways. There are too many to name, but I would like to thank the London Boater community, continuous cruiser neighbours and also the cul-de-sac at Springfield, the coal boaters, the laundrette washer women and men, the boat engineers and work people, the chandlers, the waterside pubs and boater friendly cafes and all the charities that care for wildlife on the waterways. I'm especially grateful to Jake, Jo, Rich and Eleni and Rich's parents, land friends at Merriam Avenue HW, Stephy and the late Nigel. Thanks also to the three boats, twenty-three cafes, two B&Bs, two book shops and one library, that I wrote this book in over three years, for having me.

The River Lea, Regent's Canal, Paddington Arm, Hertford Union, River Stort and all the surrounding marshes and meadows for letting me call you home. I have loved living within your world and will miss it dearly.

'The flotilla', my floating family. A most special thank you to you, my dearest boat sisters and brothers, for your friendship and all the magic, bonkers times. I will forever treasure the memories; Sam Nightingale, Abbie Valentine and her love and their boat baby, Tommy Erby and Becky Cocker and their boat baby Iris, Alice Nightingale and Ben Wadhams and boat bump, Jack Milln and Bean Downes, Bertie Dixon and Claire Fourel, Daisy Nightingale and James Fellows and boat bump, Michelle Madsen, Joe Nightingale, Matt Ingham, Ed Harty.

Mango, my boat dog, for being my best buddy and my constant. You helped me discover so much. What adventures we've had. You are a great dog. Love you boy.

My family. A very special thank you, particularly, to Mum for being mum, for teaching me how to make anywhere a home, for raising me and making me free-spirited (keep wearing all the colours). To Dad for your openness, for our chats and my sense of adventure and creativity. To Ben for always being my bestest bro and longest friend. So proud of you. Love you. Also a special thanks to Auntie Ange and Uncle Chris for being crew on my first ever day aboard.

And lastly, my boater love Ed, thank you for everything. For all the late nights you spent reading many drafts of this book and for being so supportive and patient during what felt like the never-ending editing stages. I know it wasn't easy. Thank you for saying yes to a home together that stays still. I can't wait to lay down our roots.

ABOUT THE AUTHOR

Danie Couchman is a writer, broadcaster and wanderer. She studied journalism in Nottingham and has since worked in an eclectic variety of roles, from a local radio reporter to the voice of MTV's Official Top 40. She is one of the UK's most popular voice over artists and her writing has been published in *Waterfront* and *The Simple Things* magazines.

Danie has lived in four countries, seventeen houses and three boats. She enjoys wild swimming, cooking, and adventures with her dog Mango. She is soon to be settling on land close to the sea in Devon.

Afloat is her first book.